THE FORTEAN TIMES BOOK OF

Strange Deaths

THE FORTEAN TIMES BOOK OF

Strange Deaths

COMPILED BY STEVE MOORE

ILLUSTRATED BY ETIENNE

JOHN BROWN PUBLISHING

First published in Great Britain in November 1994
by John Brown Publishing Ltd, The Boathouse,
Crabtree Lane, Fulham, London SW6 6LU, UK.
Tel 0171 470 2400. Fax 0171 381 3930.
2nd Edition, September 1995.

ISBN 1-870870-50-6

Printed and bound in Great Britain by
BPC Paperbacks, Aylesbury.

CONTENTS

INTRODUCTION

Death. It comes to us all, but to some of us it comes more strangely than others: absurdly, embarrassingly, coincidentally, fittingly or incomprehensibly...

History is littered with famous and curious casualties. The Greek playwright Aeschylus supposedly died when an eagle mistook his bald head for a rock and dropped a tortoise on it, hoping to break its shell. Attila the Hun conquered half of Europe but died of a nosebleed on his wedding night. Author Arnold Bennett drank a glass of water in Paris to prove it was safe, and promptly died of typhoid. Yet famous deaths are already well-catalogued, so we have opted instead for marking the passing of the less well-known.

Over the last twenty-odd years, the 'Strange Deaths' section of *Fortean Times* magazine has chronicled many of the peculiar circumstances in which we depart on that journey of no return. This collection gathers a number of classic tales from the column, but includes many more besides, exhumed from the bulging folders of the *FT* archives.

Is every single tale retold here the truth, the whole truth and nothing but..? Who can say?

Regrettably, in recent years the press (especially the tabloids) has developed a tendency to print unsubstantiated 'contemporary legends' as if they were fact, with names and dates and places. Possibly there *are* real events here, that only look like legend; possibly not. Although we cannot check each case, what we can do is to provide our source-references for every tale, which can be found at the end of the book.

Is there, amongst all these examples, a particularly 'Fortean' way to go? As we compile our curious collections, surrounded by creaking shelves of books, tottering piles of magazines and bursting files of clippings, we think there is. The tale is told in the *Minneapolis Star*, 21 December 1977: Police in Long Island, New York, had to use an axe to smash down the bedroom door of 70-year-old Eleanor Barry, who had been killed some days before when a huge pile of books, newspapers and press clippings fell on top of her and buried her alive.

A debt of gratitude is due to those many, many readers and supporters of *Fortean Times* who have sent us news clippings over the years, without whom neither *FT* nor this book would exist today. They are far too many to mention by name, but this collection is dedicated to each and every one of them. Thank you all. May you live long, and clip to a ripe old age!

Steve Moore

CHAPTER ONE

Cupid's Deadly Darts

We begin where it all begins, for all of us: with love, or at least with sex. Sometimes that's where it all ends too. The best way to go, or the worst? Who knows? We can't ask the dead. Take these tales as you will...the romance of death, or the death of romance.

IF LIFE IS FULL OF ABSURDITIES, so is death. On 23 November 1983, the caretaker arrived at the Condor Club, a topless bar in North Beach, San Francisco, to discover a bizarre sight. 40-year-old assistant manager Jimmy 'The Beard' Ferrozzo had been crushed to death between a trick piano and the 12-foot-high ceiling. Beneath him, naked and hysterical, was topless dancer Teresa Hill, 23.

The gutted baby-grand Steinway had been used for 20 years by topless star Carol Doda, who appeared for her act through a ceiling trapdoor from her dressing room, and descended into the club on top of the piano. After closing-time the night before, the couple had apparently decided to make love on the piano, and somehow tripped the power-switch which raised it to the ceiling. Ferrozzo died from asphyxiation due to crushing, and his companion was only saved by the cushioning effect of his body. Speculation had it that one of them may have kicked off the power at the last moment, but Miss Hill was unable to help with the details: she'd been so intoxicated she couldn't even remember getting on top of the piano.

A SIMILAR CALAMITY occurred in West Akron, Ohio, to Daisy Gladden, 20, and her lover James Daniels Jr, 26. On 17 January 1988, after indulging in drugs and alcohol, they decided to make love in a car, hidden from prying eyes inside an abandoned garage. It was all too much for 12-stone Daniels, who died in the act and trapped Daisy underneath him. With only a thin raincoat to cover her and suffering from hypothermia, she was discovered four days later when a tow-truck driver heard her screams. She was still wedged beneath the decomposing body of her naked lover.

CARRIED OFF IN THE ACT, but this time both together, were married couple Sachi and Tomio Hidaka of Chiba, Japan. Both 34, the shy couple had waited 14 years before making love for the first time, in 1992. It proved too much, and both of them died of heart attacks, though neither had any history of heart trouble.

EVEN STRANGER was the tale of Min Chou Lin, who reportedly kissed his bride to death at their wedding reception in Beijing, China, in 1987. They were both found unconscious on a sofa, locked in each other's arms, and rushed to hospital; but the girl died of heart palpitations brought on by the excitement.

ANOTHER ONCE-ONLY CASE, with grimmer overtones. Teenager Jochen had grown up together with three girls, Dunja, Petra and Christina, in a special home for deaf-mutes in Heilsbronn, Germany. In 1980, Dunja fell in love with Jochen, and one day they walked to an old deserted bomb shelter. There they made love for the first time, and Dunja cried with happiness; after which Jochen murdered her. It appears that the romance hadn't gone down well with the other two girls who, using sign language, threatened suicide if the affair continued, but offered love if it didn't. Numbers seem to have counted, and as Dunja lay with her eyes closed, Jochen hit her on the head with a bottle before stabbing her several times with a pair of scissors. All three conspirators were found guilty of murder, but only given two-year suspended sentences.

DENNIS KEOGHOE, 72, of Minehead, Somerset, wanted to make up to his wife for all the money he'd spent on prostitutes when he was younger, so he did nine paper-rounds a week. Eventually he became so exhausted that he killed himself by drinking a bottle of whisky and taking 100 painkillers.

CIRCUS MIDGET Martha Farrand, 3ft 9in, professionally known as the Vest Pocket Venus, was loved by both her partners in a high-wire act. Jealousy eventually overcame caution, and one night a fight broke out high above the audience, with both men plunging to their death in the ring.

PERHAPS CIRCUSES ARE HOT-BEDS of curious passion. Marian Paler, 36, caught her trapeze-artist husband in a compromising position, in Resita, Romania. A few hours later, Marian guffawed loudly at a critical point in the performance when her husband required total concentration, and he fell to his death from the flying trapeze: murdered by laughter.

OR PERHAPS THE CRUCIAL FACTOR is that they should be East European circuses. In 1993, Bucharest-based horse trainer Hanibal Cantori went to the stable to give his stallion Galbenus some sugar, and discovered his wife Laura having intercourse with the animal. When she confessed to regularly seeking satisfaction with Galbenus, Cantori strangled her with a silk scarf, before committing suicide.

BUT THE CIRCUS may not be so important after all: perhaps it's simply that Romania is a place of peculiar romances. We are told that beauty queen Helene Momescu, of Cetatea, had even more lovers on a string than the heroes and heroines of our previous tales: five in all. Eventually they decided on a drastic solution. The five arrived at a deserted house one night in 1978, each armed with a revolver, a bottle of liquor, a candle, and a signed letter explaining their intentions. Drinking steadily, they lit the candles and waited for them to go out; after which they would begin shooting, and the survivor would claim the girl. The last candle spluttered, the shots duly rang out… and in the morning all five were found dead. Helene was run out of town and forbidden to return.

REDUNDANT OIL BROKER Sophia Kneen, 30, was hugged to death by her spurned lover. She and commodities dealer Tim Brockman, 32, had shared a £100,000 flat in Fulham, but she had wanted to end their eight-year relationship after a series of tempestuous rows. In October 1992, after drinking with a friend and apparently joking that his plans for the evening were "murder, then suicide", Brockman returned to the flat. In what investigators suggested may have begun as a show of affection, Brockman squeezed the life out of Sophia. Bruising to her shoulders and back suggested that she had died of "crush" asphyxiation, a method of murder popularised by the 19th-century body-snatchers Burke and Hare. Brockman then laid her on the bed, wreathed her head with flowers and, some hours later, slashed his throat, chest and wrists before hanging himself from a beam a few feet away.

EGYPTIAN-BORN PROSTITUTE and rape crisis counsellor Omaima Nelson, of Santa Ana, California, clubbed her husband William to death with a lamp. They had argued about money. She then tied him to a mattress before dressing up in red shoes, a red hat and blood-red lipstick. After that she hacked her 16-stone husband to pieces and skinned him, barbecued then ate his ribs, and ground up the rest of the body in the garbage disposal. Jailed for 27 years, she told the judge she was "a warm person who wouldn't harm a mosquito".

HEALTH OFFICIALS in Istanbul, Turkey, were forced to issue a warning in 1990, about people making love on the roof during sultry summer evenings. At least a dozen people were said to die each year when, after a night on the tiles, they contentedly fell asleep... and rolled over.

PATRICIA ORIONNO of Doubs, France, became completely fed up with her husband Jean-Louis demanding too much sex. In 1988, she tried giving him an overdose of sleeping tablets, but he merely took a protracted nap. She then slashed his wrists and gassed him, but neither of those methods worked either. Then she tried smothering him, but he merely woke up. Finally, on the fifth attempt, she stabbed him eight times, and at last he died. French courts make allowances for crimes of passion, however, and she was freed.

JAZZ TRUMPETER Joe 'Pootie' Newman, who played with Count Basie and Lionel Hampton, was destroyed by his sexual appetite. Described as having "a masterly control of his instrument, a uniquely rhythmic way with the valves, a remarkable potency", he was also a keen ladies' man. In 1989 he had an unsuccessful penile implant. A build-up of pressure brought about a series of embarrassing explosions, including one in a restaurant, and internal bleeding followed. In July 1992, he eventually died of a blood clot on the brain. His last album was called *Hangin' Out*.

JOE BRAYBOY'S TASTE FOR THE LADIES brought trouble too, but this time the hand of death settled on another. Suspecting that he was visiting a lover, his wife Patricia set off with a girlfriend to find him. Driving down a street in Houston, she spotted what she mistakenly took to be Joe's grey Volvo parked in a driveway. She pounded on the house door and began to force her way inside. Hearing the commotion, a resident grabbed his shotgun and shot her dead. As her friend fled screaming down the road, she noticed Joe Brayboy's grey Volvo parked in another driveway, a few houses away.

DIONICIO VELA didn't trust his 22-year-old wife Rosa to behave when he was away from his village in Peru, so he made a chastity belt out of coarse rawhide and a padlock, for when he was away on business trips. Unfortunately the padlock was rusty, and in 1987 Rosa's skin became infected with septicaemic poisoning which eventually killed her.

CHAPTER TWO

The Font And The Altar

Romance, at least in the old-fashioned view, is followed by marriage, and marriage in turn by baptising the offspring. Of course, it doesn't always happen like that.

DESPITE HAVING BEEN HOSPITALISED by a heart attack the day before, angina-sufferer Irene Guy was determined to go through with her wedding to Brian Holmes on her 48th birthday. In June 1993, she discharged herself from hospital in Otley, West Yorkshire, and went through with the ceremony, though four hours later than originally planned. Two hours later, she collapsed at the reception and died before reaching hospital. Doctors said she would probably have died anyway, even if she had stayed in hospital, so perhaps it was worth it after all.

A NEWLY-WED COUPLE in North Carolina were given a hot-air balloon ride as a wedding gift in June 1987. The balloon became entangled in power lines, and while the wife was unhurt, the pilot suffered electrical burns and the groom was killed.

CHAPTER TWO

A GROOM and his wedding guests in Khanpur, Pakistan, celebrated by blazing away with rifles, in March 1993. When the shooting stopped, they found that five people had been killed.

THERE ARE TIMES when one suspects old man Death of devious cunning and artistic creation; or perhaps he just wants to bring low the pride of the bride. Wearing an artificial bun to enhance her natural hair, bride Thankamma Mathai, 20, looked radiantly happy as she entered the church at Trivandrum, India, in July 1977. Watched by the priest, groom, relatives and friends, she walked down the aisle and then suddenly collapsed.

As the guests rushed to her side, she gave a groan and died on the floor of the church. A doctor found the mark of a snake bite on the nape of her neck. Thankamma had worn the bun during a dress rehearsal at home the previous night, and had then placed it in a corner of the room. A small poisonous snake appeared to have coiled itself up inside the hairpiece overnight, and bitten her while she was on the way to the church... but no sign of the snake was found.

AND IF that isn't enough to convince you that weddings can be hazardous to your health, consider the following. A couple from Shanxi province in northern China gave the equivalent of £2 as a wedding gift to their nephew in June 1991, while other relatives gave £4.80. The sums are small, but China is poor; and the difference is what counts. Unable to bear the other relatives' scorn at their paltry gift, and worried about future wedding gifts for other nephews and nieces, Yang Baosheng hanged himself after his wife Qu Junmei drowned herself in a vat.

IMMEDIATELY AFTER his marriage at Council Bluffs, Iowa, in June 1979, 23-year-old Greg Cundiff was stricken by nerves and heat. He hit his head on the altar steps and never regained consciousness.

SURVIVING THE WEDDING and sorting out the gifts may not be enough in themselves; there's still the reception to follow. In September 1990, a joint reception was held for a double wedding when two brothers got married at Ramtha in Jordan. As the brides were dancing and singing with a group of women guests, the dance floor collapsed beneath them. There was a cesspool under the floor into which they all plunged. Thirteen were killed, including both brides; 10 women from the same family were among the dead. Both bridegrooms were in another room at the time, and escaped the tragedy.

JOHN BLUE, 47, was drowned while being baptised at Lake Cochituate, Minnesota, in September 1983, when he lost his footing. Said the pastor – like Blue, a non-swimmer – "Maybe God wanted him."

FROM ACCIDENTS TO VIOLENCE: they were still partying 11 hours after the wedding of Max Hoffmann, in Traunreut, Bavaria, in October 1991. Unfortunately Hoffmann, 39, went berserk when his camera failed to work, and gave his father a black eye. His mother Astrid then stabbed her son to death with a kitchen knife in front of the bride and 40 wedding guests.

NO ONE TOLD German-born bride Amy Weltz that it's an old tradition in Australia for newlyweds to smear wedding cake on each other's faces. When new husband Chas pushed a slice into her face at their reception in Brisbane in September 1993, she hit him over the head with a wine bottle. He died instantly.

ZHANG JIAHUA, 44, was arrested in February 1992 when railway officials searched his bundle, in Shanxi province. Inside it they found the body of a woman who had died two years earlier. Zhang had dug her up in the southern province of Sichuan, and transported her across China for eight days, so that she could be 'married' to a man who had died a bachelor. According to Chinese tradition, dying unmarried is unlucky, and posthumous marriages are frequently arranged. Zhang had been paid the equivalent of £40 to act as 'matchmaker for the dead'.

CHAPTER THREE

More Than Anyone Can Stand

What's normal to some may be continuing hell to others, and some people have remarkably low breaking points. Once the threshold has been crossed, the over-reaction that follows occasionally reaches berserk proportions.

MODEL STUDENT Huang Yashuo, from Wuhan, in China's Hubei province, hoped to become a scientist, and studied hard every evening. Unfortunately she became very frustrated when her 82-year-old grandmother disturbed her by insisting on watching television while she was studying. Things came to a head on 10 January 1993, when her parents were away and Huang was revising for a final examination. Granny switched on the TV. Huang took a hammer and smashed in the back of Granny's head, until she was quite dead. Then she wrapped the body in two bags, put it under the bed, and carried on studying.

FOR MICHAEL S. ALLEN, 48, of Markham, Illinois, it wasn't so much the television itself as the programme. His 88-year-old mother insisted on watching the Bill Cosby

Show. As Allen couldn't stand the series, he shot his mother several times with a .22 calibre revolver in July 1986 and left her dying on the living-room floor while he went off and turned himself in to the police.

THE BREAKING POINT for Marlene Love, 39, came in October 1991 when husband Douglas, 38, settled down to watch his fifth football game of the day on satellite TV in Calgary, Alberta. She shot him in the back of the head with a rifle. She told police: "There was no food in the house and I kept asking him to give me some money and the car keys so I could go to the store; but he kept saying 'Shut up! Can't you see I'm watching a game?'"

MUSIC AS WELL AS TV can get on some people's nerves. In Bangor, Maine, Earl Losier Jr shot dead four people in March 1988, including his brother and a pregnant woman. The reason, he said, was "because he was taking cough syrup and because they were playing the stereo too loud."

ANOTHER MUSICAL MURDER comes from Messina, Italy. Giovanni Mancuso was an amateur pianist who practised daily on his grand piano. The main drawback was that his repertoire consisted of only one piece, and his annoyed neighbour Pietro Pettinato eventually shot him for it. The tune Mancuso had been repeatedly playing was Chopin's Funeral March.

NATURAL NOISE ANNOYS too. Near Perth, Australia, in March 1991, drug addict Joseph Taylor, 22, got fed up with the coughing of his brother Dale, 16. So fed up, in fact, that he locked him in the boot of his car, doused it with petrol, set it on fire and burned him to death. "I could hear my brother yelling and screaming but he'd just coughed one time too many," Taylor told police.

GRAVELY ILL Thomas V. Fowler Jr., 76, died in hospital in July 1989, yet the autopsy showed the cause of death as 'blunt neck trauma'; a shorthand way of saying strangulation, beating, or a combination of the two. Fowler had been sharing a room with William Fitzmeyer, 43, at the Winthrop Community Hospital in Massachusetts. Fitzmeyer had been unable to sleep because Fowler kept snoring, so he killed him for it.

SHOPKEEPER Luigi d'Alessio, 47, shot his doctor dead in Foggia, Italy, when the doctor said he couldn't cure his cold.

PSYCHIATRIST Oscar Dominguez, 45, shot dead a woman patient in his office in Sao Paolo, Brazil, as she told him about her sex life. At his trial he explained: "I couldn't take those nutcases any more..."

THOMAS CORLETT, 58, a senior executive officer at the Department of Employment, had strict ideas about where the German mustard should be placed on the dining table. His Austrian wife Erika, 63, failed to comprehend this, in spite of 15 years of marriage. In December 1985 an argument broke out. "It was her fault," he said. "I always placed my newspaper on one side of my plate, the mustard on the other. But she moved my paper and put the mustard in its place instead, saying, 'that's where I want it, and that's where I will put it.' She started shouting and kept on and on about the paper. She raised her hand and I thought she was going to hit me. I just grabbed her by the throat and we fell to the floor." After that, he strangled her.

CHAPTER THREE

A MAN STABBED his wife 219 times after an argument over milk. "He told me he had killed his wife," said Patrolman John Simcoviak of Joseph Fallar Sr., 61. "He said she would stack the refrigerator full of vegetables, hiding the milk, and he wasn't going to take that any more."

IN GERMANY, Walter Juergens, 19, was served up eggs at every meal by his new wife Elfriede, 18. He got so fed up with it that he left home. When he decided to return in January 1990, Elfriede immediately fried up some eggs for him. He shot her dead, remarking after his arrest: "I used to like eggs..."

ROYAL NAVY ENGINEER Derek Guy had a trivial argument with his wife Sharon over a slice of toast and marmalade at their home in Market Harborough in July 1988. He thereupon ran into the road, lay down and waited for a car to run over him. A few minutes later, a Ford Escort ran over his head, killing him.

IN ST LOUIS in December 1986, Nathan Hicks, 35, became enraged when his younger brother Herbert used six rolls of toilet paper in two days. There were still two rolls left in the carton, but Nathan shot Herbert in the chest with a .22 rifle and killed him.

A SCIENCE TEACHER in St. Marcel, Normandy, accused a 15-year-old boy of stealing a light bulb in March 1978. He kept the boy in after school, and the next morning told the class about the incident. As he did so, the humiliated boy stood up, pulled out a revolver, and shot him dead. He then went into another classroom and put a bullet through his own head.

AFTER SCHOOL in Cesena, Italy, 10-year-old Andrea Casanova always went back to the home of his friend Roberto Pulzelli, and helped him with his maths homework. Roberto's 18-year-old sister Pasqua felt her little brother was relying too much on outside help, so after several scoldings she decided to put an end to it, by taking her father's shotgun and blasting Andrea to death.

AT KREFELD in Germany a 34-year-old university chemistry professor was furious when an 18-year-old schoolboy beat him at chess in May 1988. In a curiously misplaced act of vengeance, he killed the boy's 12-year-old sister with a bottle.

AT TOKYO'S TAKUSHOKU UNIVERSITY, students at a karate club kicked Tetsuya Mori, 19, to death and severely injured another student in July 1986. The victims had failed to wash their uniforms.

PANTELIS VIZONIS, 54, stormed out of the taverna in the village of Palea Vigla, Greece, in March 1985, when a friend jokingly accused him of never buying a round of drinks. Shortly afterwards he returned with a shotgun killing two friends and the taverna's owner. Then he returned home and shot dead his wife and two other friends who tried to restrain him.

PERHAPS SOME FORETHOUGHT could prevent such tragedies; but then again, forethought can also be the problem. Salvatore Romano, 65, from Agrigento, Italy, decided that his daughter's fiancé was too ugly for her. So when 30-year-old Calogero Lumia turned up at his house in March 1993, Romano opened the door and shot him with a pistol.

He explained to police: "If he'd married my Anna I'd have had to look at him for the rest of my life."

A 13-YEAR-OLD BOY was handing out slices of pizza to homeless men in a squatter camp by the Miami River in Florida in September 1993. He was quite definite that it was one piece each, so when one of the men took two, the boy shot him dead.

KNIFE IN HAND, Chen Bohong of Liuzhou, China, was slaughtering his pig in October 1987 when taxman Sun Taichang turned up and presented him with a £1 pig-tax bill. Outraged, Chen decided to slaughter the taxman instead. He was duly executed for his crime.

UNIVERSITY GRADUATE Dong Huibo, 24, doesn't appear to have done anything at all to provoke his death on a Shanghai bus in August 1992. He was sitting there minding his own business when the woman bus conductor began hurling insults about the shape of his bottom. She then progressed to swearing at him, slapping his face and breaking his glasses, and making a grab for his privates. As Dong tried to protect himself, she stood back and aimed a kick between his legs. Panicking, Dong tried to escape through a window, but the driver, also a woman, stamped on the accelerator and sent him flying. After that, she stopped the bus, and both conductor and driver stood there watching him die in the street with blood pouring from his nose and ears.

CHAPTER FOUR

A Ridiculous Way To Go

We think of death as 'The Grim Reaper', but some demises are so ludicrous we begin to suspect the old boy of having a sense of humour. One can almost hear an eerie chuckle as the following tales unfold...

ALEXANDER MITCHELL, 50, a bricklayer from King's Lynn, Norfolk, died laughing in March 1975 while watching the TV comedy *The Goodies*. He had recently eaten, and after 25 minutes of laughing on a full stomach his heart failed while he was watching a fight between a set of bagpipes and a black pudding.

IN OCTOBER 1992 Mrs Dorothy Johnson's two-year-old great-grandson offered her a jelly sweet before taking off his hat to show her his new, extremely short haircut. The 72-year-old widow from Birmingham found this so hilarious that she burst into uncontrollable laughter, and choked to death on the sweet.

FEAR OF SNAKES did for Jose Sanchez, 65. In January 1993. Sanchez was snoozing peacefully in a hammock when his wife Maria threw a toy rattlesnake at him. He was so frightened he died of a heart attack.

MORE CURIOUS STILL was the case of Charles Lecuere, 55, of Bordeaux, France, who had always had a great terror of rats. He and his wife Monique, 52, kept their marriage fresh by surprising each other with occasional special treats. In June 1988 Monique bought a brunette wig and left it on a shelf in the bathroom. Before she could put it on, Charles went to clean his teeth, without his glasses. He mistook the wig for a huge rat, which he thought had crawled in through the window and was about to attack him. He also died of a heart attack.

JOBLESS DANIEL PITIORET, 43, decided he wanted to die, and asked his friend Thierry Dierick to do the deed. Dierick, 29 and also jobless, wasn't keen, but Pitioret offered him £6,500 and told him he'd give him a letter to prove he'd been asked to do it. He then threatened to commit suicide anyway if Dierick didn't help. So, in March 1993 they went for a last supper at the best restaurant in Bourg-en-Bresse, in south-east France. Pitioret paid the £200 bill by cheque and they vanished into the night. Later, Pitioret's body was found in a wood, his head almost blown off from behind by a shotgun.

Police found his ID card and a cheque stub made out to Dierick, on which was written "payment for a contract to kill me." They immediately arrested Dierick and, despite his letter, charged him with murder. The cheque bounced.

MICHAEL TOWNSEND ended it all the other way up.

The fit 60-year-old from Bath was found dead on the beach at Woolacombe, North Devon, in April 1982. He was wearing only his underpants, and was kneeling with his head buried in the sand. He had been seen earlier walking out to sea and apparently making no attempt to swim, but it was assumed he'd returned to shore. Half an hour later he was found head down in the sand.

A DISPUTE among a group of Filipino men over that age-old question 'Which came first, the chicken or the egg?' ended in tears. On the side of the chicken were Georgio Santos and Tomas Ja, a pair of barbers from the town of Tamban. The egg-men were Jose Martas and Francisco Ferre. Thinking he'd won, Ja cried out: "You are fools! What I say proves that the chicken came first!" Unfortunately his argument is not recorded, but it appears to have upset his opponents. They pulled out pistols and shot both the barbers dead.

A 29-YEAR-OLD FILIPINO man stabbed his elder brother to death and wounded a drinking companion in a dispute over whether Imelda Marcos was prettier than the Princess of Wales. The dead man supported Princess Diana.

AIR ACE Colonel William T. Whisner, 65, who shot down 24 enemy planes over Germany and Korea and won the DSC three times, died in July 1989 after being bitten on the cheek by a gnat in his garden at Pineville, Louisiana.

MOUNTAINEER Gerard Hommel also met his Maker in an ironic fashion. The veteran of six Everest expeditions, Hommel was changing a lightbulb in the kitchen of his home in Nantes, France, in October 1993, when he fell off the ladder. He cracked his head on the sink and died.

SOMETIMES, it seems that Nature herself is the joker. In February 1982, David M. Grundman of Phoenix, Arizona, went out into the desert and fired repeatedly into the trunk of a giant saguaro cactus for target practice. The large pitch-fork-shaped cactus is Arizona's state plant and an endangered species. As Grundman fired off his last round, the heavy upper section of the cactus, 23 feet long, toppled over and fell on him, spearing him to death.

IN JANUARY 1989, 73-year-old Robert Hamm fell rear-end-first into the dustbin he kept on his front porch in Rochester, New York. He spent the next three days jammed up to his armpits, with his legs sticking in the air. On the first day an 11-year-old newspaper delivery girl waved to him and said hello; he waved back and mumbled something, and she went on her way. On the second day the postman saw his hand move, but ignored it. On the third day, the newspaper girl's mother went to investigate and found him still there. By that time he'd died of heart failure.

KEEP-FIT FANATIC Steven Ray from Sheldon, Birmingham, had a fourth floor flat in Hong Kong. In September 1988 he locked himself out, so he decided to abseil down the side of the apartment block from the roof and get in through the window. Rather than go down by rope, however, he was using a piece of string. The string snapped and he fell 50 feet to his death.

AN UNNAMED MAN of 56 tricked his way into a house in Alicante, Spain, in May 1991, by claiming to be a sewing-machine repairer. Once inside, he grabbed 18,000 pesetas (about £80) and ran off. As the woman chased him, he tripped, swallowed his false teeth, and choked to death.

MOUTH ORGANIST Ramon Barrera of Mexico, once famous for playing 'the world's smallest harmonica', was giving an exhibition performance in Iguala in January 1994, when a moment of excitement caused him to swallow the harmonica and choke to death.

SHOP MANAGER Claude Jules, 53, of Abbeville, France was so eager to try on his new toupée that he got the special glue out in his car and donned the wig there and then. He sat back to admire his handiwork and took out a cigarette. Unfortunately glue fumes were ignited when he tried to light it, turning the car into a fireball.

HOSIERY KNITTER Hardial Singh, 41, took a bath at his home in Leicester in November 1992. Afterwards, he tried to balance his backside on a broomstick while opening a window. He slipped and impaled himself on the broom handle, and fled the bathroom screaming. He was taken to hospital where an operation was performed to remove his injured bowel, but he died two weeks later when blood clots reached his lungs.

AN UNNAMED MAN of 35 from Austin, Texas, became entangled in a garden hose and strangled himself while trying to get free. He was found in a field behind an Austin food plant in May 1983 with the hose wrapped round his waist and chest.

SCORNED WIFE Cecille LeDoc of Nice, France, was so angry at how her husband Daniel was running round with other women that she hit him around the head with her pet turtle. He died in June 1993 of his injuries, but the turtle survived.

A NAKED MAN running across New York's Brooklyn Bridge in May 1993 singing "Oh what a beautiful morning!" was run over by a car and killed.

IN MARCH 1988 a motorist from Commerce, California, strapped his teddy bear into the passenger seat but didn't bother to do up his own seatbelt. He was killed when his car spun off the road and fell 35 feet. The teddy bear was unharmed.

AS A SICK JOKE, we are told that disc jockey Ashwari Sharma told listeners in Calcutta to drop a radio in their bath-tub for an "LSD-like high", in January 1994. He faced manslaughter charges after 20 teenagers followed his advice.

MOST LUDICROUS in its sheer pointlessness is a strange tale from June 1984, when a Chinese newspaper published a photograph of three smiling soldiers posing on a railway track, their backs to a speeding train which killed them a split second later. The paper, *China Law*, did not explain why the photographer, a fellow soldier who was presumed to have jumped clear in time, failed to warn them of the approaching danger.

CHAPTER FIVE

Snow Jobs

When the cold hand of death settles on our shoulder, could there be a more appropriate place to be than in the midst of snowfields and ice?

SNOWBALLS can be deadly. Tony Bowers, 7, of Lawley Green, Shropshire, was killed by a snowball in January 1980. With his brother and a friend, he had been rolling up a giant snowball on a ridge near his home, with the intention of letting it roll down the hill. Unfortunately, the five-foot-wide, 3cwt snowball got stuck, so Tony tried to free it by clearing the snow in front. He did his work too well, and the snowball rolled over him, pinning him face down in the snow. Although the other boys kicked the snowball to pieces and freed him, he died of crushing and asphyxiation.

TONY'S DEATH was described as a million-to-one freak accident, but exactly the same thing happened to Robin Morrell, 12, of Hereford, in April 1989. His snowball was only four feet wide, but it too rolled on top of him and pinned him face down. His brother found him with only his feet sticking out from the snowball, but he suffocated before he could be freed.

EVEN MORE BIZARRE was the accident that befell Sherry Gados, 34, in December 1988. Apparently having lost her keys, she tried to break into her own house, in Dayton, Ohio, through the pantry window. Why she didn't rouse her husband John, who was sleeping inside, is far from clear – as is the reason why she was wearing only underwear and socks. Nonetheless, it appears that the window closed on her foot, trapping her and leaving her dangling upside down. An element of farce entered the tragedy when she was spotted by next door neighbour Wilma Johnson, but ignored. For some inexplicable reason, Wilma managed to convince herself that Sherry was nothing but a shop-window dummy hung outside the window, and only investigated some hours later when she saw her still there. By that time, Sherry was covered with snow, and had died of exposure.

FIVE GERMAN GLIDER PILOTS over the Rhine Valley in 1935 were suddenly caught in the updraughts of a gigantic storm-cloud, and decided to bale out before their planes were shaken to pieces. Alas, the same updraught caught all five parachutes and sent them hurtling several hundred feet further up into the air. After a while, they began to descend, only to be caught in another updraught... and so on and on repetitively for several hours, before they finally reached the ground. By that time, four of the men had frozen to death.

APTLY-NAMED Karl Winter brought his death upon himself in 1984. The 19-year-old poacher had a cunning plan to foil the gamekeepers in the snowy woods in Rovereda, Switzerland: back-to-front boots. Making prints with the heels and soles the wrong way round, he fell down a crevasse. Search parties set out to find him, went the wrong way, and he died before he could be rescued.

DURING THE SEVERE winter of January 1981, New York police entered the Bronx apartment of Jessie Smalls, 47, and found her encased in a block of ice. A water pipe had burst and flooded the place, and they had to chop the ice away before they could recover the body.

A 48-YEAR-OLD NURSE, Laverne Landis, and her companion, Gerald Flach, drove into the snow-covered mountains from their home in St Paul, Minnesota, in 1982 to wait for the spacemen to land. They lived in their car for a month, surviving on vitamin pills and water. The police checked on them every week, but felt unable to interfere. Unfortunately the flying saucers never showed up, and Laverne died of exposure. Gerald, almost dead from starvation, was rescued.

BEAUTIFUL GHISLAINE SANCHEZ, 37, left Paris for Mont Blanc in October 1990, seeking her inner self. Practising a form of Buddhist meditation which involves exposing oneself to extreme cold and standing under freezing waterfalls, she was spotted by climbers as she ran round the mountain. She told them she was trying to prove that existing in temperatures of -30 degrees would toughen her. A few days later, she was discovered 6,000 feet up a glacier, having apparently abandoned her clothing altogether and sitting naked in meditation. Unsurprisingly, she had frozen to death.

RECLUSIVE MISER Joseph Heer, 89, had his power cut off in January 1986. He was found in bed, fully clothed, in Washington, Pennsylvania, having died of hypothermia. In an open safe and two steel boxes nearby, police found $200,000 in cash.

CHAPTER FIVE

PIERA RUTELLI, aged 40, was driving through a tunnel near Genoa, Italy, in February 1991. A large icicle fell from the tunnel-roof, penetrated the roof of her car, and killed her.

STEPHEN READER, 25, of Morden, London, was obsessed with cold for three years. He was convinced that a new Ice Age was coming, and during that period he seemed to be preparing for it. He would only eat cold food, and if given a hot meal he would place it in the refrigerator until it was frozen solid before consuming it. He refused to work anywhere but in freezer centres, or at night, and insisted on taking his holidays in cold places. In January 1989, he went on holiday to Resolute Bay in North Canada, but found it wasn't cold enough for him. After that, he thought about going to Alaska, but ended up in Iceland instead. There he set off for Klanders mountain, dressed only in a tracksuit and boots, and with no equipment. He was found five days later at the foot of the mountain, without shoes or socks, lying huddled in a ditch. He had died of exposure and hypothermia. Curiously, for a man so obsessed with ice, he had been put into care 10 years previously... for an arson offence.

CHAPTER SIX

Revenge Of The Machines

And now, the malevolence of inanimate objects. From seemingly purposeful vengeance to mere inhuman spite, the machines have it in for us...if we don't actually end up in them...

THE UP ESCALATOR at the New York Telephone Company office, installed in 1974, had a history of problems and bizarre behaviour. In 1982, 30 people were injured when the chain-drive broke and the escalator went into reverse, and there had been almost weekly complaints in the few months leading up to the moment when Emma Niskala stepped onto the machine for the last time, in September 1987. The 35-year-old accounting clerk had risen a few feet when the step on which she was standing gave way. Swallowed by the escalator, she fell three or four feet into the machinery. The upward motion of the surface steps coupled with the downward motion of those underneath sucked her in still further. Police tried to free her with their hands and with automobile jacks, but she was crushed to death among the churning machinery before they could get her out.

CHAPTER SIX

A STEEL CABLE snapped at a sawmill in Chester, Texas, in 1983. As the broken cable whipped across the mill at neck height, it decapitated the owner and three employees, and injured a fifth man.

RUNAWAY Darren Gooch, 17, had left home after a row with his parents, and was staying at the Cora Hotel in Euston, London, early in 1988. While there, he boasted to night porter Stanley Rogerson about the way he had got three free cans of Coca-Cola by tilting the hotel's drinks machine. The next night he tried it again, and the 800-pound machine, perhaps rather put out at being robbed in this way, toppled over. It took four men to lift the machine off him, but the crushing had caused brain damage, and he died after being in a coma for nearly three months.

Gooch was said to be the first person in Britain to die in this fashion, but such deaths were widespread in the USA during the 1980s. Either tilted for free drinks or shaken when they failed to produce a can or the right change, the insulted machines struck back to kill 11 American servicemen or their relatives, and injure 39 more; at least four civilians had been canned in a similar fashion besides.

EVEN IN THE GREEN English countryside, the machines lie in wait. Plastics factory owner Michael Davis, 53, decided to bore a hole in the garden of his isolated home at Ranmore Common, near Dorking, Surrey, in April 1991. Instead he ended up planting himself. He was using a large corkscrew drill attached to a lawn-mowing vehicle, but as the drill was activated his clothes got caught up in it. The soil drill then proceeded to dig itself into the ground, taking Davis with it. When he was discovered by his wife Marion, only his head remained unburied. She called the emergency services, but though firemen battled for two hours to rescue the mutilated gardener, they were unable to save his life.

FARM WORKER Edward Russell was found unconscious beside his tractor in Broadreed Farm in Hampshire, completely naked except for his shoes and socks. The 'power take-off gear' (an evocative phrase) was thought to have injured him and stripped him of his clothes. He died in hospital in February 1975.

DEATH CAME FROM THE AIR for construction worker Ramon Jose Rodriguez, 23, who was employed at a site in Miami, Florida, in December 1988. While he was innocently going about his business, a portable toilet toppled itself off the fourth floor of the building and fell on him. He was pronounced dead about an hour later. The toilet was on rollers, and was thought to have been blown down by a gust of wind.

WOOL-MILL OWNER Paul G. Thomas, 47, was operating a pin-wheel dresser machine, which winds woollen yarn from a large spool onto a smaller one. Somehow he fell onto the small spool and was tightly bound to it as 800 yards of yarn were automatically spun round him. He suffocated before the accident was discovered.

SOME MACHINES KILL, but others are capable of killing and then disposing of the body as well. Thomas Maguire of Cahir, Co. Tipperary, worked for Shift-It Ltd, a garbage disposal company. In January 1993, 47-year-old Maguire arrived at a supermarket in the town of Tipperary to collect a skip full of stale vegetables and shop refuse, a job he had done regularly for the last three years. A couple of hours later, the supermarket reported Maguire missing, although his garbage-packing truck was still outside, with its motor running. Investigators uncovered his grisly end. Maguire had been standing on the skip and had got sucked into the truck with the rubbish, where he was packed to death as the garbage-truck compressed and crushed him.

IN MAY 1988, George Kenyon was finely diced when he was dragged alive and kicking into a shredding machine at a factory in Haslingden, Lancashire. He was feeding plastic into the cutter when his overalls became tangled, and he was chopped up by a giant rotary blade before a horrified colleague could turn it off.

IN A SIMILAR accident, Richard Charters, 40, was using a machine which had operated safely for 15 years at a bed factory in Trowbridge, Wiltshire, in November 1983. It shredded bales of fibre used in mattress making. He was dragged through trap doors by a conveyor belt into the shredding machine and beaten to death by flails.

TYRONE MITCHELL'S DEATH in March 1993 was described by an investigating officer as "one of the most gruesome things I've ever seen in police work." 34-year-old Mitchell was cleaning large machinery at a food plant in Selma, Alabama. He was inside a giant meat-grinder when it started up unexpectedly and minced him to death.

KILLER MACHINERY can be quite specific in its target. The Prado family were returning by bus to Santa Ana, California, from a trip to Mexico in May 1992. As the bus sped along the San Diego Freeway, four-year-old Ramon fell asleep with his head on his mother's lap. At Oceanside, 70 miles south of Los Angeles, one of the bus's tyres blew out. Steel cables from the tyre thrashed a three foot hole in the floor of the bus, and then one of them snaked up, wrapped itself around Ramon, and dragged him down onto the freeway. He was crushed by the bus wheels and other cars, but his mother was quite untouched, and no one else was injured.

IN JAPAN in 1981, Kenji Urada was killed when a robot at the Kawasaki factory where he worked mistook his head for a component that needed tightening up.

ADELAIDE MAGNASCO, 80, went on holiday in Aosta, Italy, in August 1993. Retiring for the night, she pulled down the cupboard bed from the wall of her chalet, got in, and died when it suddenly snapped closed again. She was found by her son Paulo, crushed between the mattress and the wall.

IT SEEMS MACHINES can get emotional, even peevish. Chess Grandmaster Gudkov outwitted and checkmated a computer three times in a row at a public tournament in Moscow in March 1992. The next time he touched the machine it got its revenge by electrocuting him.

THE MAXIM that "cleanliness is next to Godliness" seems all too true. In Boston, Massachusetts, laundry worker Alfredo Castro was inspecting a large clothes dryer in January 1991. As he did so, a load of wet laundry dropped on him and pushed him inside the machine; the lid slammed shut and the machine started automatically. Castro was trapped in the spinning drum for six minutes and died from suffocation after being tossed around in a temperature of 180° Fahrenheit. His body was eventually tipped out with the washing, "looking like a boiled lobster".

THE MOST LUDICROUS LAUNDRY-DEATH comes from the western Chinese province of Xinjiang, where two schoolteachers, Aierguma and his wife Paheerguli, hired a 16-year-old nanny in July 1991. Being relatively affluent, they owned a washing machine and, one day in their lunch hour, taught the girl how to do the laundry with it.

Before returning to work, Aierguma told her: "After finishing the washing, don't forget to bathe the baby." She did exactly as she was told; after finishing with the clothes, she put the one-year-old boy in the washing machine and turned on the power. The baby drowned. The teachers were said to "regret hiring an uncultured nanny."

CHAPTER SEVEN

The Long Arm Of Coincidence

"It's nothing but coincidence." We've all said it at some time or other, but is there more to it than that? Are there self-replicating events? Or do things appear as fiction the first time around before emerging into reality later?

IN NEW ORLEANS more than 100 lifeguards threw a party in April 1992, to celebrate their first ever year without a tragedy. While they were busy partying, one of the guests, who was not a life-saver, fell into the swimming pool fully-clothed and drowned... even though four lifeguards were supposed to be on duty at the time.

AMERICA'S SAFEST TEENAGE DRIVER, Michael Doucette, 16, from Concord, New Hampshire, won a contest called 'Operation Driver Excellence', held in Detroit. He received a $5,000 scholarship, a trophy and the use of a 1989 Dodge for a year. He was driving the Dodge on 23 February 1990 when he crashed head-on with a car driven by Sharon Ann Link, 19, on her side of the road. Both were killed. Police said that Doucette appeared to have fallen asleep at the wheel.

LIFE IMITATES ART. In 1837, Edgar Allan Poe wrote *The Narrative of Arthur Gordon Pym*, in which four shipwrecked and starving sailors drew lots to pick who should be eaten by the others. The loser was called Richard Parker. In 1884, the yacht Mignonette was shipwrecked in the south Atlantic. Four sailors survived for 20 days with only two tins of parsnips and a captured turtle. One of them was a 17-year-old boy who was eventually killed and eaten by his fellow crew members. The survivors were finally rescued and returned to England, where two of them were sentenced to death for the murder, but immediately reprieved. The victim's name was Richard Parker.

OPERA STAR Marie Collier came to fame when she stood in for Maria Callas in *Tosca* in 1966. In the last act of the opera the heroine leaps to her death. *Tosca* had also been Collier's last performance before a meeting at her London home with her financial adviser about a new tour of America, in December 1971. During the conversation, she opened a balcony window and fell out, plunging 30 feet to her death in the street below.

DOUBLY COINCIDENTAL was the death of 65-year-old bingo caller Michael Cave. He idolised comedian Tommy Cooper, who died in mid-performance on television. Cave had seen it happen and told his wife that that was exactly the way he wanted to go too. In June 1992, he was 15 minutes into his bingo routine at a club in Reading when he called "Number eight...Pearly Gates", and then collapsed. He was rushed to hospital, but was dead on arrival.

A NAME ITSELF often seems sufficient cause for the events that follow. Amelia Smoke, 22, was visiting a friend in Chicago in August 1901. The friend's son was smoking. Picking up a cigarette, Miss Smoke said: "It is becoming a fad to smoke cigarettes, and I will light this one up and take a puff for fun." The fun didn't last long, as a spark dropped in the folds of her dress, and she didn't notice the flames until they reached her face. She was dead before the fire could be extinguished.

IN AUGUST 1987, an 18-year-old girl from Egham, Surrey, died in hospital after being crushed under her horse, which had collapsed from a heart attack. Her name was Jennifer Squelch.

THEN THERE ARE CASES where an event is commemorated, and the commemoration itself leads to repetition. Mrs Sue Alton, 33, of Dorking, Surrey, went riding with friends along Pilgrim's Way, a footpath in Abinger Hammer, near Dorking, in March 1987. Her horse bolted and she was thrown head-first against a five-foot-tall stone monument. She was killed instantly. The monument had been erected in 1873 to mark the spot where the Bishop of Winchester, Samuel Wilberforce, had been killed while reading the Bible: he fell on his head when his horse put a hoof in a hole.

SOME PEOPLE simply should have known better. In the village of Moosbrun, Austria, the brass band played an annual spring concert. In 1987, during the Klevenhuller March, 71-year-old conductor Johann Kolominn collapsed and died on stage of a heart attack. The following year, new conductor Franz Gessner, 70, included the same march in the programme, in memory of his predecessor. As the audience watched in horror, the conductor's baton froze in mid-air and he, too, died of a heart attack.

MOPED RIDER Erskine Lawrence Ebbin was knocked off his machine by a taxi and killed in Hamilton on 20 July 1975. It was the same taxi, with the same driver, carrying the same passenger, that killed his brother Neville, on the same day of the previous year. Both brothers were 17 at the time, and had been riding the same moped in the same street. Only one thing prevented history repeating itself precisely: the time of day was 50 minutes different.

EQUALLY BEWILDERING is the story of Onder Akgun, a dentist at Elazig State Hospital in Turkey. Akgun was driving on a religious holiday with his wife and three children when a truck crashed into his car repeatedly from behind killing his son, who was asleep on the back seat. The truck driver said it was an accident. Some years later, in September 1991, Mr Akgun drove to Bursa on the same religious holiday. A car crashed into them repeatedly from behind and killed their daughter, who was sleeping on the back seat. The car driver said it was an accident. Not surprisingly, Akgun asked why, if both were accidents, they were crashed into several times on each occasion.

GIVE A CHANCE EXAMPLE and the world will respond with an instant, and all too appropriate, demonstration. In October 1987, a picnic was held on the banks of the crocodile-infested Zambesi river, in the Caprivi strip between Botswana and Zambia. As postmaster Kobus Slabbert was warning children to stay out of the water, a giant crocodile grabbed him by the leg and dragged him screaming down the bank. He surfaced twice before disappearing. His body was never recovered.

DEATH STALKED Barton Road, Stretford, Lancashire, on 8 January 1974. Two women, quite independently, collapsed and died while walking there, within five hours of each other. Maud Richardson, 69, and Hannah Bradbury, 76, were both said to have died of natural causes.

SALVATORE AND FLORENCE Graziano stayed together rather longer after they met at a dance in Chicago in 1932: they married a year later and remained inseparable for more than 50 years. In October 1984 Salvatore, now 77, had a heart attack and was taken to Chicago's Illinois Masonic Hospital for treatment, where 75-year-old Florence visited him daily. One morning she arrived at the hospital and told a nurse that she wasn't feeling well, so she was taken to a doctor's office for a check-up before seeing her husband. Unknown to her, Salvatore's condition had deteriorated overnight, and he died while Florence was being examined. At precisely the same moment, 9.09am, Florence flopped into the doctor's arms and died of a heart attack. It was said that she suffered only a mild heart attack, which shouldn't have been strong enough to kill her; and there was no way that she could have known of her husband's death at the same time.

COSMIC JUSTICE can often masquerade as coincidence. Vincent Orr, 38, served four years in jail for the murder of his girlfriend Gillian Callaghan on New Year's Day 1985. He admitted repeatedly hitting her head on the concrete floor of their home in Radcliffe, Manchester, following a drinking session and a row. In the summer of 1991 he went on holiday to Corfu with his new girlfriend. Taking an early morning dip on his first day there, he smashed his head on some rocks and died in hospital several hours later.

FIVE MOUNTAIN RESCUE POLICE helping to make a film about the dangers of avalanches in the French Alps were swept away and killed by an avalanche in December 1980. TV cameramen looked on in horror, but were helpless to do anything.

MIKE STEWART, 31, president of the Auto Convoy Company, Dallas, Texas, was filming a movie about the traffic dangers of low-level bridges in April 1983 when the truck he was standing on passed under a suburban bridge and killed him.

CHAPTER EIGHT

Death Chains

Naturally, deaths do not always come singly, or even in pairs; all too frequently they cluster in large scale accidents or even larger extinctions. But occasionally, there seems to be a chain of causation where one death leads to another, and another.

GRIM DISASTERS OF THIS KIND happen at least once a year in many parts of the world. Five farmers followed each other to their death in a manure pit in Menominee, Michigan, in July 1989. Carl Theuerkauf, 65, his sons Carl Jr and Tom, grandson Daniel and friend Bill Hofer were attempting to clear a drain in the 13-foot manure pit, which was only a foot deep in dung at the time. Hofer went in first and collapsed suddenly, overcome by the colourless, odourless methane gas given off by the manure. One of the Theuerkaufs went in to save him but he was also overcome in turn. Then the others followed, one after another, until all five were killed...leaving only Theuerkauf's third son, Bill, who had already been badly injured in a car accident three years previously, to run the dairy farm.

CHAPTER EIGHT

THE WATER PUMP failed at the foot of a well owned by a family in Rawalpindi, India, in April 1979. One man went down to investigate, but didn't come up again. A second member of the family went down to investigate and didn't reappear either. And so it went on, one after another, until 12 members of the family had lowered themselves into the well and been killed by poisonous fumes given off by the pump.

THE MONTOYA FAMILY had a 13th floor apartment in the Caballito district of Buenos Aires. They were away in October 1988, but they had left their poodle Cachi behind. The balcony of the apartment faced the street, but it was thought to have a secure wall. Somehow, though, Cachi got over it and plummeted to the street. He landed on the head of 75-year-old Marta Espina, instantly killing both her and himself. A crowd of sightseers gathered around the incident, including Edith Sola, 46, who was unable to get close and had to stand in the middle of the street. There she was knocked down and killed by a bus. Shocked by the carnage, an elderly but unidentified man who had seen both incidents collapsed with a heart attack and died in the ambulance on the way to hospital. A neighbour remarked: "There were bodies everywhere. It looked as if a bomb had exploded."

SOMETIMES WHOLE FAMILIES are struck down together. The beach at the industrial town of Porto Vesme is frequented by the locals, even though signs warn that swimming is prohibited. In August 1993 Margherita Smenghi, 15, took to the water and was sucked into an unprotected factory water-intake. As she cried for assistance at the mouth of the 14-foot-diameter pipe, her eight-year-old sister Teresa jumped in to help; she too was dragged into the intake.

Brother Gabriele, 6, and his friend Mauro Salaris, 11, tried to help, but they too were sucked in. Word was brought to the children's mother, Pinella, 34, as she was reading a book on the beach. Naturally enough, she did what she could, diving off a wooden bridge to try to save them. But as they clung to her neck, she too was drawn in... to be followed, inevitably, by father Georgio, 42, who worked at the plant, and was called away from his fishing to help. The six bodies were eventually found piled on top of one another, halfway along the 30 yard intake, bruised and cut by the pipe walls. It was believed that whirlpools caused by the high tide had formed at the mouth of the pipe, and pulled them in.

IN AUGUST 1984, Vebi Limani was struck dead by lightning near his home on Sara Mountain in southern Yugoslavia. His father, a brother and an uncle had suffered the same fate in the previous few years, while a sister had been invalided by a lightning strike.

WHILE THE DEATHS may be of the same sort, they can occur at much wider intervals. Alasdair Munro, 39, set off in his boat on 15 June 1993 to search for his fox terrier, Frisky, which he believed had gone round a nearby headland, near Tarbet, on the west coast of Sutherland in Scotland. As friends and neighbours watched from the shore, his boat capsized, and he was lost... making him the seventh member of his family to drown in the past 35 years.

In 1958, schoolboys Donald and John Munro drowned with their uncle, also called Donald, when their small boat foundered off the island of Handa. In 1972, Alasdair's father, Alistair, was lost while lobster fishing. In 1974, his brother Angus was washed overboard from a fishing boat near Oban, and in 1987 his brother Cathel drowned with a friend while crossing to Handa to shear sheep. Alasdair's mother was killed in a car-crash during a blizzard in 1990; he was a back-seat passenger at the time.

A CLASSIC TALE from 1839. In May, a group of men were building a log house in Gibson County, Ohio, when a quarrel broke out among them. One of the men in the argument was high up the wall and chopping wood from the corner of the building; he threw his axe at one of the men below, which hit him in the abdomen, splitting it open and causing his swift demise. The man who had thrown the axe lost his balance as he did so and fell over backwards, tumbling to the ground and breaking his neck. Stunned by these developments, a group of men who were rolling a log up the hill toward the house let go of it, and it rolled back on them, killing three and wounding and bruising others. As the original newspaper source quaintly puts it: "In the secret dependencies of crime upon crime, we may well conceive that there is often a succession, imperceptible to human observation, as that made so horribly manifest in the case stated."

IN THE UKRAINE, a funeral wake turned to drunken revelry and then disaster in June 1988. The funeral, in the village of Zabolotye, was for a man who had died of poisoning after drinking black market industrial spirit. Exactly the same rotgut was served at the wake, with the result that 10 guests died and 80 had to be taken to hospital.

IN ANGTHONG, 60 miles north of Bangkok, Thailand, Yooket Paen, 57, slipped over in the mud of her farmyard in May 1991. As she fell, she grabbed a live electric cable, and was fatally electrocuted. Later the same day, her sister Yooket Pan, 52, was attempting to explain the accident to her neighbours when she too slipped in the mud; almost inevitably, she grabbed the same live cable, and followed her sister in death.

THERE ARE PLACES which attracts Death again and again, reaping his crop one by one. The sleepy village of Woodseaves, Staffordshire, with a population of only 500, is such a place, being shaken by a series of fatal accidents and bizarre suicides in 1989-1990. Vicar Roy Harrison was the latest victim, hanging himself in the stairwell of his vicarage in November 1990, shortly after the death of his mother. A week earlier, factory worker Darren Holmes had gone to his former lover's house on Bonfire Night and burned himself to death. The previous month, fencing contractor Ray Langham had died when his Jaguar was involved in a car crash. Before that, John Clapham, a fruit and vegetable merchant from the village, had been killed on a business trip to California, when he was hit by a truck after his car broke down. A few months earlier still, Roy Lawrence died of kidney failure when he was given the wrong type of blood during surgery. And finally, weapons expert Gerald Bliss was testing a "fail-safe" weapons system for the Ministry of Defence when he was killed by an exploding shell. The village postmistress remarked: "It's as if there's a curse on the place."

SPEAKING OF CURSES, consider the following tale. On 30 August 1990, Simon Craven, 28, was fatally injured when his car collided with two parked vehicles on the Eastbourne seafront. He was the eighth Earl of Craven, and his death was the latest in a series of events seeming to fulfil a 350-year-old curse on the family, supposedly the work of a pregnant servant girl. The first Earl was William Craven, a soldier who received the title in 1626. Since then, no Earl has lived beyond the age of 57. Simon Craven's elder brother Thomas, the seventh Earl, shot himself in 1983 in a fit of depression, aged 26. His father died at 47 from leukaemia. His grandfather died at 35 during a wild party on a yacht. Although the family are said not to believe in the curse, it is also thought to centre on the Craven ancestral home, Morewood House in Berkshire, which was sold after the seventh Earl's suicide. The latest owner of the house, Dr Robert Reid, committed suicide shortly before Simon Craven's death.

CREDIBILITY IS STRETCHED in our concluding tale of Hungarian artist Hans Kinnow from Budapest. In the late 1930s, he painted a portrait of a millionaire's wife. He'd just finished it when his model slumped dead of heart failure. His next sitter was a wealthy bank director, who died a few days after the picture was completed, and the next subject, the daughter of a doctor, died too. Kinnow vowed never to paint again, but a year later he fell in love. Just before he and his fiancée were married, he agreed to paint her portrait; she died of pneumonia within a week. Kinnow became an odd-job man, and was found dead in a cheap Budapest lodging house in April 1938. Beside him was a crayon sketch dated the previous day – of himself.

CHAPTER NINE

Second Time Around

From tales where death strikes repeatedly, we move to those where it seems the first chance was missed and only made up for on the second attempt. There could be dress rehearsals for our exit from the world...

LEBANESE-BORN AIR STEWARD Mohammed Wafiq Zarif and his English wife Kathleen Denham divorced in 1985 but remained friends. Shortly before returning to Lebanon in December 1990, Zarif took out 12 life insurance policies worth 1.1 million pounds; four days after his arrival in Beirut he was reported killed in a car crash. Apparently acting in good faith, Denham went ahead and claimed on the policies, as well as on his British Airways pension. But the death was faked, and in January 1991 Zarif phoned his ex-wife. She later told police that Zarif had threatened to have her murdered by a friend if she didn't press ahead with the claims, but as the insurance companies couldn't get confirmation of his death from Lebanon, only one of the policies was paid. Denham obtained £15,000, of which she sent

£10,000 to Zarif. He went out and bought a car with his ill-gotten gains, and in July 1991 he crashed it... and this time he really was killed.

DEATH GETS A SECOND CHANCE most often in road accidents, as the following tales show. In September 1990, an unnamed woman escaped serious injury when her car hit the central reservation of the M25 near Brentwood, Essex. Dazed, she wandered safely to the hard shoulder but then turned back, apparently trying to make her way back to her car. As she did so, she was mown down by a tanker and a truck and killed, in what then became a multiple pile-up, with at least two more lorries jack-knifing.

CHARLES MILLBANK, 25, crashed into an electricity pole on the A127 near Brentwood, Essex, in January 1993. The car plunged over an embankment, but he escaped unhurt. As he scrambled back up the slope, he touched the 11,000 volt cable trailing across the grass and was killed instantly.

A FIERCE GUST OF WIND blew Vittorio Luise's bubble car into the river Sele near Naples. Luise, 45, managed to break a window, climb out and swim to shore. There a tree blew down and killed him.

WOODROW KREEKMORE had a narrow escape in February 1985 when his car skidded off an icy road and slammed into a telegraph pole outside Chickasha, Oklahoma. He climbed out and strolled into the road to hitch a ride. He had only walked a couple of feet when the pole keeled over behind him and struck him dead.

GERARDO GREGORIO JR of Aklan province in the central Philippines attempted suicide in February 1989 by drinking insecticide, but was saved by his neighbours. He wasn't at all pleased to wake up alive in hospital, pulling a dextrose tube out of his arm and stalking out. When he returned home, he cut down three of his neighbours with a machete and wounded three more. Other residents then put a stop to his murderous rampage by hacking him to death.

ALSO IN THE PHILIPPINES, Enrique Quinanola, 21 and unemployed, tried to hang himself at his home in Cebu City on 11 September 1990. His relatives cut the rope and took him to hospital. As doctors prepared to sedate him he escaped, ran to a nearby restaurant, grabbed a knife and slashed his wrists. Police saw the incident and tried to subdue him, but he put up such a struggle that they shot him, first in the leg and then in the chest. He died a few moments later. Remarkably, Quinanola's family then filed a complaint with the government's Human Rights Commission, alleging violation of his civil liberties.

GEORGE SCHWARTZ, 54, was alone and working late in the office of his factory in Providence, Rhode Island, in December 1983. A huge explosion virtually flattened the building and sent flames racing through the wreckage. Only one wall was left standing, but the blast swept Schwartz clear of falling masonry and flames, dumping him on the front steps. After treatment for minor injuries and shock, he returned to the factory to try to salvage his business files. The last remaining wall collapsed and killed him.

FROM TALES WHERE the same form of death is avoided once and then met with later, we move to a cluster where an entirely different demise replaces the first attempt. In

October 1993 a women-only commuter train was struck by lightning in Bombay. Believing the stationary train to be on fire, a large number of women (variously given as 23, 35 or 49) jumped down on to the tracks, where they were then mown down and killed in semi-darkness by another train.

AN UNFORTUNATE FISHERMAN, in August 1977, set up his rod on the banks of the Rio Negro in Amazonia. His fishing line caught in a tree, and as he tried to free it, he struck a bees' nest. The infuriated swarm went on the attack, and the man leapt into the river to escape. He was devoured by piranha fish.

FRUSTRATED at the first attempt, death (or the gods) can switch attention to another person entirely. In July 1991, 65-year-old Chan Wai-fong set up a small shrine at her son's home in Hong Kong to give thanks to the gods for her daughter's lucky escape from a road accident. As she was praying in the street outside the apartment block, she was killed by a falling bag of cement.

IOANNIS PHILIPPOU, 50, set himself on fire while huddled over a heater in his home in Kato Deftera, Cyprus, in January 1990. To douse the flames, he ran out of the house and jumped into a reservoir, where he drowned.

CHAPTER TEN

They Brought It On Themselves

There are many ways in which one can be responsible for one's own death: an act of stupidity, a plan that goes wrong, a long-held obsession. We may not see the ultimate consequences, but the universe somehow responds to our desires...

NO ONE REALLY KNOWS what Arthur Sharland was getting out of it, but his turn-on was electricity. The 77-year-old pensioner from Shepherd's Bush, London, would sit in an armchair with two wires running from an electric socket attached to his bare chest with crocodile clips, and flick on the power. Eventually it killed him, and in August 1989 he was found dead of electrocution; although from the mass of tiny scars on his chest, some many years old, it seemed that he'd been regularly plugging himself into the mains for much of his life.

EIGHTEEN-YEAR-OLD Ian Stewart of Maidstone, Kent, had two wishes. One was to fly in a helicopter, the other he only mentioned to his mother after painting his bedroom entirely in black and white: he wanted a coffin to sleep in. Two days later, in January 1992, he was injured in a road accident, and got his first wish: he was flown to hospital by helicopter. Shortly thereafter, he died, and gained his second wish. To round off the set of coincidences, when his mother got home from the hospital, she found that his bedside clock had stopped at 10.46am: the exact moment Ian had died in hospital.

POLISH-BORN Kazimerz Symanski had been a prisoner in the Second World War, and never got over the experience. He turned his north London flat into a cell, placing bars on the windows and sleeping in a wooden box in the form of a cage, which had a grilled door he could chain shut from inside. The flat was even more like a prison camp in that it had no electricity or running water, and he used the kitchen floor as a toilet. The windows were nailed open because he feared being gassed; he had also told a neighbour he thought he was being attacked by radiation. 81-year-old Symanski was thought to have lived in these conditions for five years. When police eventually broke down his barricaded front door in April 1993, they found that the conditions, and the open windows, had got the better of the old man: he had died of bronchial pneumonia, caused by hypothermia.

THERE ARE PLANS which, fine in principle, go wrong in practice. In Grahamstown, South Africa, a man asked police to watch his house while he was out of town, saying he would be back on 12 January 1992. The police became suspicious on 30 December 1991 when they saw lights being switched on and off in the supposedly empty house. Suspecting a burglar, an officer went to the back door of the house and, when a door suddenly opened, let loose with his gun… killing the homeowner, who had returned early and forgotten to notify the police.

KENNETH SUTHERLAND'S PLAN went terribly awry. The 38-year-old auto-worker from Sumpter Township, Michigan, had a nice little sideline growing marijuana plants in his garage. The only trouble was, the local teenagers occasionally broke in and stole his plants, so Sutherland decided to rig up a booby trap. He nailed a shotgun to a chair and ran a wire from the trigger to an outer screen door, so the gun would go off if the door was opened. One day in June 1993 something went wrong, and he seems to have forgotten his own trap. The shotgun blasted him in the thigh, and though he managed to drag himself 60 feet to the house and dial the emergency services, he was then unable to say anything. He bled to death before help could arrive.

ANOTHER SILLY BLEEDER was Nitaro Ito, 41, a restaurant owner from Osaka, Japan, who was running for election to the House of Representatives in 1979. He asked friends to beat him up and then stabbed himself in the thigh, hoping for voter sympathy and the publicity which would result from running his campaign from a hospital bed. Unfortunately he stabbed too deeply, and died from loss of blood during the 20-yard walk from his car to his house.

ONE EXPECTS more style from the Japanese, and that was certainly provided by Masahiro Oki, 64. He was a 36-dan martial arts grand master, an expert on yoga, held three degrees in Western medicine and others in Oriental medicine, and was reputed to be the only samurai not to have prostrated himself before Emperor Hirohito, even though he had once been his personal physician. He and his students had moved to Pesaro, Italy, where he continued his yogic practices. Oki was said to have reached a level of attainment where the elements are regarded as a form of illusion. In August 1985, he began to meditate on this by wearing a lead-weighted jacket and assuming the lotus position underwater. He drowned during his fourth immersion, and his students were unable to resuscitate him, despite using "ancient samurai methods".

STUDENT DAVID REYNOLDS described in an essay how he was shot dead at a motel in Hartford, Connecticut, where he worked as a night clerk. A few nights later, in June 1979, he was shot by a mystery intruder. He had even got the time of his own death right.

BE CAREFUL WHAT YOU WISH FOR... In December 1976 Sam Davidovitch, 60, sipped a glass of wine and asked the band to play his favourite song in a restaurant in Tel Aviv. "This is how I want to die," he said, "with a glass of wine in my hand while the band plays my tune." Then he got up to dance with his wife, sang the words... and dropped dead of a heart attack.

JOHN BUTTERICK, A RESEARCHER at West Virginia University, was obsessed with long life. While studying in Canada, he had spent six months ingesting BTH, a chemical used in food packaging to retard spoiling, but later he believed he had found the substance that would allow him to live for 200 years. The substance was warfarin, sometimes used in small quantities as an anti-coagulant, but best known for its use as rat poison. In January 1980 he was found lying on his bed in his apartment, having bled to death, with blood covering his clothes, the mattress, a glass, the kitchen floor and the bathroom. Butterick's quest for immortality had been cut short at the age of 33.

LOUISE RAMOS, 64, was arrested for shoplifting in San Diego, California, in October 1983. As a protest, the sexagenarian vowed to hold her breath "until I turn blue". True to her word, that's exactly what she did, and died in hospital a few days later.

IN MEXICO it may be routine to swallow worms with tequila, but on America's west coast an unnamed 29-year-old man went one better in 1979. Having drunk half a pint of whisky, he then swallowed a newt as a dare. Unfortunately he chose to swallow a newt of the *Taricha granulosa* family, which is a hundred times more poisonous than its east coast cousins, and contains enough toxin to kill 1,500 white mice. He died a few hours later.

IF NOT SO DARING, some people are prone to imagine themselves as something they're not. Sometimes, the fantasy has its weak spots. Walter Hallas of Leeds reckoned he was a hard-man, but was terrified of going to the dentist. Tormented by toothache in November 1979, he decided on a cowboy-style cure, and asked workmate Mark Waldron to punch him on the jaw and knock the tooth out. After some hesitation, Waldron duly obliged with a right jab; whereupon Hallas, 26, fell to the ground and hit his head on the concrete floor, fracturing his skull. He died in hospital six days later.

SOMETIMES, WE ASK FOR IT. On Halloween 1988, Michael Tyree turned up at a bar in Boston, Massachusetts, dressed in a spooky costume and carrying a noose. As a prank, 41-year-old Tyree wanted to stage a fake hanging, but the bar owner wouldn't let him. He left, but returned an hour later after the owner had gone off duty for the night, and proceeded with his stunt. Something went wrong with his harness, and he choked to death before a group of delighted revellers who had no idea he was dying before their eyes. He was eventually cut down and rushed to hospital, but couldn't be saved.

THERE'S A CERTAIN SATISFACTION to be obtained when the subversion of a venerable institution is suitably punished. Spanish police nicknamed the burglar who had made 12 successful raids on Pyrenean ski-lodges Santa Claus, as his method of entry was to slide down old-fashioned wood-fired chimneys while the lodges were locked up for the summer. In 1985, on his thirteenth caper, things went wrong for Jo Montpol, aged 26. He slid down a chimney in Viella, but got jammed fast in an extractor fan, and starved to death.

MILWAUKEE BOY Paul Gleffe, 12, taught himself to lose consciousness to amuse his friends. In May 1979 the stunt went wrong when he died after collapsing and hitting his head on the school playground.

A MAN WAS KNOCKED DOWN by a car in New York in July 1977, but got up uninjured. A bystander told him to lie down in front of the car again and pretend he was hurt so he could collect some insurance money. He did so, and the car promptly rolled forward and crushed him to death.

CHAPTER ELEVEN

By Their Own Hand

Many and peculiar are the reasons why people decide to kill themselves; often the ways they choose to do it are even stranger. Sometimes the well-deliberated death appears to become part of the cosmic process, and the act of self-immolation an artform in itself.

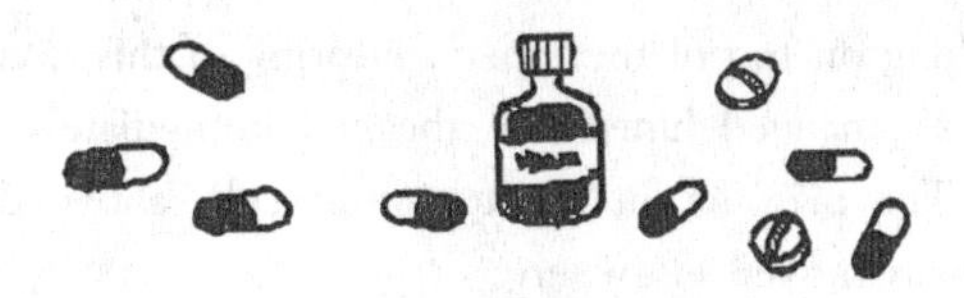

MISS CHEUNG YUEN-MAN OF HONG KONG died because her forehead was too high. Soon after leaving secondary school she went to see a fortune teller who looked at her face and told her that she would bring bad luck to her friends and family, and that it would be most appropriate for her to work in a funeral parlour as a make-up artist for corpses; that way she would live longer. She didn't take his advice, but as the years passed she became obsessed with the prediction. By the time she was 22, she was almost completely sleepless, spoke frequently of the devil and being persecuted, and made offerings to the dead. When she changed her job, her employer was killed on her first day at work. A month later, on 24 March 1992, she jumped from the building where she lived, landing on her "mis-shaped" head and died instantly.

EVIL FORTUNE, or perhaps a strange destiny, also stalked Saughton Prison, Edinburgh, in July 1976, where ouija-board sessions were taking place among the prisoners in cell 13, known as the condemned cell and conveniently placed next to the old execution room. The participants believed they had contacted the spirits of executed criminals and eventually the ouija board named prisoner Thomas Rankin, 41, as marked for death. That night he began a lengthy screaming session, calling for his mother and eventually becoming so agitated that he was removed to a solitary cell. The next morning he was returned to the ground floor cell 13, where in the afternoon he was found to have hanged himself.

Soon after, the ouija board announced further deaths, coming "one on top of the other". Hearing of this, Matthew Collins, 27, hanged himself in the cell immediately above cell 13. The prisoner in the top floor cell, above that of Collins, was moved elsewhere.

EVEN MORE OBSESSED with the past (or perhaps the past was obsessed with her) was the aptly-named Sandra Killington, 21, of Barking, Essex. According to her diary, she had fallen in love with a businessman called Thomas Fanshawe, who lived in the 1600s, believing that he was somehow still alive and having a relationship with her in 1981. Finally, she wrote in her diary: "I'm going to kill myself so we can go back to live as we used to." She then lay down in front of a train while holding her four-year-old daughter Nicola. The child struggled free of her mother's arms at the last moment; Sandra died for her strange love.

A CITROEN CAR was the object of 22-year-old Michael Bennett's passion. One night in 1991 he overturned it on the way back from the pub to his home in Driffield,

Humberside. A friend, following in another car, helped him right it and tow it home. Bennett was in tears and kicked the car, then went down on his knees to kiss it better, sobbing "Sorry, car". Then he remarked: "I want hanging for that." Several hours later he was found dangling from a tree, on the same tow-rope he'd used to bring the car home.

IN MARCH 1981, an unnamed man was found hanging from a tree in Los Angeles. A car was parked nearby, bearing the licence plate 'Black Dog', and a leather whip was draped over the tree branch. The man was dressed entirely in black, with a black felt hood. He was also wearing a Frankenstein monster mask.

FONG YEE PIN, 10, a schoolgirl from Penang, Malaysia, hanged herself in her bedroom in 1990 after her family killed her pet chicken for lunch.

DO STRANGE SUICIDAL FORCES drift through time and space, to settle unseen and unwelcome where they're least expected? Could such a thing have happened in January 1888, when Rear-Admiral Versturme dined at home with his wife in Arwenack Mansion, near Falmouth? After the meal, they retired to the drawing room where Mrs Versturme declined to sing, but offered to play the piano. As she opened the instrument, the Admiral began to stir up the fire with a small poker. When she looked round, he was standing with an alarming expression on his face and the red-hot poker in his hand. By the time servant Ellen Davis arrived in the room, the Admiral was lying on the floor, "struggling and banging about", having stabbed himself deeply in the abdomen four times with the hot poker. Davis got the poker from him, whereupon Versturme began hugging the lighted lamp that was on the floor. Extinguishing the lamp with a rug, she summoned a doctor. The Admiral was still alive when he arrived, frenzied and suffering from "a paroxysm of suicidal mania". He was also bleeding from the mouth, where he'd swallowed several pieces of broken glass and china. Nothing could be done, still less explained, and he died shortly afterwards.

AND WHAT DO YOU DO if, driven by the same impulses, you don't have the same mechanical competence? It seems that if you can't build your own, any machine will do. Trisha Williamson, 33, of Cape Town, South Africa, was depressed after losing her job in April 1993. Only 4ft 6in tall, she climbed into her dishwasher and was scalded to death.

DEEPLY RELIGIOUS Donald Allanson, 41, of Norton, Yorkshire, became upset in 1985 when he heard that a close friend was having an affair. Such was his hurt that Allanson tied a chainsaw between the branches of tree, jammed the throttle full on, and walked into it, beheading himself.

THE DRILL WAS PREFERRED by both Joe Boothroyd and Colin Rees. In 1987, Boothroyd, 71, of Westbourne in Sussex, was depressed about angina pain, so he drilled a hole in his heart. In 1990, Rees, 63, of Barry, South Wales, stabbed himself four times with a knife and scissors, before finishing the job by drilling a hole in his head.

DURING A ROW with his wife in 1993, Christopher Daley, 37, of Stanford in the Vale, Oxon, used a nail gun to shoot a two-inch bolt into his brain. Simpler still for Dennis Widdison, 61, a depressed epileptic of Newark. In May 1987, he used a hammer to drive two five-inch nails into his head, and still survived long enough to pull them out afterwards. Pharmacist Gregory Feld, 45, of Toronto, did away with the sharp instruments altogether. In February 1990, he was found sitting in his blood-soaked Jaguar, having beaten himself to death by hitting his head with a tyre iron.

ALSO IN TORONTO, Franco Brun, 22, turned the very item that was supposed to help him through his troubles into a fast ticket out of them. In 1987, Brun was rushed to hospital from the detention centre where he was serving a 15-day sentence. The authorities had provided him with a pocket Bible the size of a deck of cards, which he'd promptly swallowed. It became so firmly lodged in his throat that doctors could only peel off individual pages rather than remove the whole thing. A tracheotomy was performed, opening his windpipe, but by then it was too late.

RELIGIOUS FERVOUR fuelled William Robins of Romford, who'd internalised the Scriptures until he was convinced he was Jesus Christ. On 2 July 1988, dressed only in his underpants, he spent an hour and a half balanced on a rail of the Mercantile Credit building in Holborn chanting "God give me strength" and telling onlookers that "he had screwed up his mission the first time around and this time he was going to get it right". Explaining further, he said "if I die today I will rise up and be the second Christ. If I don't die today I will become the Devil." Then he jumped, falling 11 floors and departing this life with multiple injuries.

ALSO SEEKING A SECOND CHANCE were 51 despairing peasant girls in Jiangxi province, China, who died in 15 separate group drownings in 1988. In what might be seen as a magical act designed to present a good image to the gods, many of the dissatisfied teenagers dressed in their best clothes before hurling themselves into lakes. They were hoping to be reincarnated as rich, sophisticated city women.

MASS SUICIDES by pensioners are even rarer. Concerned about their future in the afterlife, a number of wrinklies started taking their own lives in Jiangsu province, China, in March 1993. According to Chinese tradition, the dead should be buried, so they arrive whole in the otherworld, but the local government decreed that anyone dying after 1 April should be cremated. More than a hundred old people killed themselves to ensure burial, using sleeping pills, drowning, hanging and jumping off bridges. One pharmacist reported that a group of pensioners invaded his premises demanding sleeping pills, because they had to beat the deadline. When he told them he'd sold out, they head-butted his drug-cabinet before rushing into the street and throwing themselves in front of a passing lorry.

IN EAST LONDON, South Africa, a crowd of bystanders gathered in 1979 to watch a man on top of a cliff threatening to throw himself over the edge. As he teetered, a 64-year-old stepped forward from the crowd, announced that he would show him how it was done, and promptly plunged to his death. The first man was so startled and horrified that he fainted, and was dragged clear by the onlookers.

CHAPTER TWELVE

It's The Voices

"The Devil made me do it..." An excuse always to hand when we act out of character, but sometimes it seems there's an invisible cast of thousands ready to whisper in our ears.

CONVINCED THAT HER HUSBAND Felix had become possessed by the cartoon character Mickey Mouse, Roseann Greco, 52, ran over him repeatedly with her car, in the driveway of their home in West Islip, New York. Convicted of manslaughter, she went to jail for a 5-15 year spell.

GLORIA GONZALES, a 14-year-old girl from Poteet, Texas, was shot dead in February 1981, and Ruben Gonzales Estrada was arrested for her murder shortly afterwards. Estrada had an excuse, however: God and the Martians were to blame. Nineteen-year-old Estrada told the officers who arrested him that "he was ordered by God to do this work" and that he had "five more to go" to complete the assignment. Obviously more than a little confused, he later changed his story, saying: "The Martians made me do it."

SPACE CADET Lester Donaldson of Toronto believed that he was being controlled by aliens. Referred to Dr Joseph

Johnson, a psychiatrist, he revealed that he had direct contact with the aliens, and that they'd used "flying saucer rays" to put a computer in his brain. Johnson diagnosed paranoid schizophrenia, then lost track of the patient for two years. When Donaldson turned up again, this time accompanied by his wife Myrtle, he claimed the CIA was controlling him; Myrtle apparently believed his every word, and could not be persuaded otherwise. Donaldson, who was not deemed certifiable, received some treatment but declined the follow-up day care. Eventually, in August 1988, 44-year-old Donaldson took a knife and attacked police who were calling at his home. They shot him dead.

FORMER NAVAL OFFICER Peter Dowdeswell, 60, suffered from periodic bouts of religious obsession after being told 25 years earlier by a naval chaplain that he had been selected for a "spiritual purpose". In January 1979 he received two messages from God. The first came in as he and his wife Marie were driving home to Eastbourne after a holiday in Ireland: God told him to go to Windsor and see the Queen. When Marie objected, he pushed her out of the car and continued on his own. She was picked up by another motorist and taken to Uxbridge police station. Eventually Dowdeswell arrived at Windsor Castle and presented himself at the police house there, saying he had received a message from God "on the direct line" and that he had a divine duty to save the Queen. Forewarned by their colleagues at Uxbridge, the Windsor police arranged for him to be reunited with his wife at the Castle Hotel, where they took a room.

There Dowdeswell received his second message. He began by trying to convert Marie, apparently because she was obsessed with worldly goods. Then God told him to kill her. He strangled her, and then forced tissues and water down her throat to symbolise the body and blood of Christ; after which he phoned the police and gave himself up. He told detectives he had asked God: "Do I really have to kill her? Is this my duty? He said it was my duty." Dowdeswell pleaded guilty to manslaughter, and the court recommended he be sent to Broadmoor.

JOAN RACNIL OF PERTH, Western Australia, was committed to a mental institution in June 1986 after she slit her husband's throat and cut his body into small pieces. She said the angels drove her to do it.

IN SHEFFIELD LAKE, Ohio, 23-year-old Michael Trofimov joined a religious group in 1988. Not long afterwards he announced that Christ was in him, and began speaking in tongues. This didn't seem to straighten out his life, however, as he was awaiting trial on a stolen property charge. There didn't seem to be any divine guidance for his driving, either, as he managed to crash his car into a railway train. He escaped with minor injuries, but shortly afterwards went into convulsions. Taken to hospital by his uncle, with whom he was living at the time, he refused all medication. The following night, after Michael had agreed that attending the religious meetings might not be a good idea, his father came to visit him. All seemed well, and Michael told everyone how much he loved them before his uncle and aunt went out for a cup of coffee. When they returned, they found Michael talking in tongues and screaming for God... and strangling his father, John. The elder Trofimov didn't survive. Michael pleaded not guilty to murder by reason of insanity.

LEST IT SHOULD BE THOUGHT that one religion alone is responsible, here's a tale from another. Allan Swindon,

23, of Redcar, became obsessed with Buddhism while suffering from depression, but doesn't seem to have understood it very well. He thought that the fierce-looking Protectors of the Doctrine mentioned in the Buddhist text, *The Diamond Sutra*, as standing on either side of the Buddha, were actually demons. Worse still, he told his doctor that they had pronounced a curse on him, intending to drive him insane. His father burned the book on Buddhism that he had been reading, but to no avail. Swindon was found drowned on the beach at Redcar in October 1989.

IN CAMDEN, NEW JERSEY, 31-year-old Doris Triplett was cleared by reason of insanity in January 1991 after telling a psychiatrist that her teddy bear had ordered her to kill her three sons.

FINALLY, A VOICE OF A DIFFERENT KIND. Claudia Vernicci was attending the burial of her husband in Florence, Italy, in August 1987, when she heard his voice coming from the coffin. Rather than being the sign of a miraculous resurrection, it turned out that the voice was being thrown by ventriloquist Paulo Dino, 32. Dino, who had been trying to break into showbusiness, said: "I only meant it as a joke, I never really thought Mrs Vernicci would think it was her husband speaking. I thought she'd get a good laugh from it." Dino's sense of humour was misplaced, to say the least; Mrs Vernicci keeled over, clutching her heart, and died of shock. The budding ventriloquist was arrested.

CHAPTER THIRTEEN

The Madness of Cults

If individuals can perform strange acts under the influence of direct messages from the beyond, then it's hardly surprising that even more weirdness crops up in the hothouse atmosphere of cults, sects and full-scale religions.

KEITH HAIGLER AND HIS WIFE Kate seized a bus full of passengers at Jasper, Arkansas, in July 1982. They were members of a cult led by The Messiah. The couple wanted to draw attention to their religion and threatened to shoot the passengers unless a TV crew was sent. Cameras were rushed to the scene by helicopter, and they announced that they were going to kill themselves, but their religious faith would enable them to be resurrected after three days. As police ordered them to drop their weapons and thousands watched the live broadcast, Haigler appeared to be preparing to shoot his wife. She got in first and shot him in the head, then turned the gun on herself. The three days passed, but there was no resurrection.

ONE CAN ONLY WONDER at the strength of belief that defies death, but the Haiglers were not alone in having it. Rodrigo Maneja, 33, of Cebu in the Philippines, headed a cult called 'Kahal ha Masiyac', which believes it will survive a nuclear war. In August 1985 he gathered hundreds of followers and spectators to demonstrate that he could return from the dead within four hours. His brother-in-law poured petrol over him and ignited it, as Maneja called out to the crowd that "Elohim will protect me." When four hours had passed with no signs of returning life, police took his charred remains to a funeral parlour. This doesn't suggest much hope for surviving nuclear catastrophe, but Maneja's mother said she would "continue worshipping the God who asked my son to sacrifice his life."

HEAVEN IS THE ATTRACTION in our next tale too. In May 1987, Sun Yingpeng started a 'sacred sect' in eastern China, saying he was looking for a select band to travel to paradise. Sun, from Lixin county in Anhui province, enrolled six other people, and they assembled on the bank of a river to wait for a magic boat to come and take them to paradise. They sang and danced, but the boat failed to appear, so the group walked into the river, where six of them drowned. Hong Yinglao, whose husband and daughter-in-law were among the dead, was rescued by fishermen. As the only survivor, she said later: "I won't do this kind of thing again..."

SOME 53 HILL-TRIBE VILLAGERS in the Vietnamese hamlet of Ta He committed mass suicide in October 1993 with flintlocks and other primitive weapons, believing they would go to heaven. The suicide was inspired by a local man called Ca Van Liem, who had proclaimed himself 'king'.

TWO MILLION PEOPLE gathered round the sacred lake of Kumbakonam, near Madras in the southern Indian state of Tamil Nadu, in February 1992, seeking to wash away their sins. Forty-seven people were killed, some when a wall they were standing on collapsed under their weight, the rest trampled to death by a stampeding crowd. Some witnesses explained the stampede as resulting from the crowd pressing forward to bathe during the 45 minutes which astrologers had designated as particularly auspicious. Others had a stranger tale to tell: that the state's chief minister, Jayalalitha, who had played the roles of Hindu goddesses in popular films before turning to politics, was present, and that the crowd had stampeded for a glimpse of him taking a ritual bath.

INDIA SWARMS WITH MYSTICS and gurus, many of whom are all too eager to show off their attainments to the general public. A 'godman' called Khadeshwari Baba claimed yogic powers and announced that he would enter a 10-foot-deep pit near the town hall in Gorakhpur on 20 October 1980, and remain there in deep meditation before emerging alive after 10 days. District officials were present when he entered the pit, and something of a show was arranged around the event by another yogi, 'Pilot Baba', who was believed to have served in the Indian Air Force before retiring from the world.

More than 1,000 people, mostly women, gathered round the pit, making offerings of cash, gold and valuables worth several thousand rupees, all of which mysteriously vanished along with 'Pilot Baba' at the end of the event. Still, the 10 days passed, and Khadeshwari failed to emerge from the pit. A man was lowered in to find out what had happened, and reported an overpowering stench; from the decomposed state of his body, it was obvious that Khadeshwari had been dead for several days.

CHAPTER THIRTEEN

IN TANZANIA, NINE YOUTHS who were members of the Pathfinders, a scout-like organisation, were in a canoe on their way across Lake Victoria to a religious festival on an island. They were accompanied by a Seventh Day Adventist cleric, and were part of a flotilla making the journey in October 1993. According to witnesses, they decided to prove their faith by walking on the water, as a result of which all 10 of them drowned. Not surprisingly, the church claimed it was merely a tragic accident, caused when the canoe capsized, but police spokesman Alfred Gewe stood by the testimony of the witnesses, saying: "They tried walking on the water like Jesus, but they all drowned."

THERE'S A MYSTERY surrounding our next case. In December 1975, the body of Jean-Paul Maurice, 20, was found beneath the walls of the Dinant citadel, an old fortress in Belgium. He was assumed to have died of natural causes, and was buried immediately. However, in February 1976, another young man, Michel Piersotte, was found dead near another fortress, Namur Castle; an examination showed that his internal organs had been crushed "by an amazing force". Noting the similarities in the place of death, and discovering that both young men had been members of the Children of God sect, founded in California in 1968, the police decided to exhume Maurice's body. They discovered that he had died in exactly the same way as Piersotte but, apart from the suggestive fact that both men had expressed a desire to leave the sect, there seemed to be no explanation for their deaths.

DURING A PRAYER MEETING in western Java in February 1988, a 35-year-old woman stamped to death 10 children aged under seven, including some of her own.

VILLAGERS IN THE PHILIPPINES cut off the heads of a religious leader and his wife in May 1979 after challenging them to prove there was life after death.

A SNAKE APPEARED under a peepul tree in Hapur, near Delhi, in February 1992, and was taken by Hindus as a divine sanction for plans to build a temple at the site. A group of Muslims objected, and the ensuing street battle left eight dead. The snake, however, left the scene as soon as the clash erupted.

500 PEOPLE WERE CRAMMED together on a floating shrine in July 1993 during a Roman Catholic festival in the Philippines. As they prayed, the vessel capsized, hurling the worshippers into a river north of Manila. More than 240 were killed as drowning pilgrims clawed and fought each other in their efforts to 'save' themselves.

FINALLY, COLLECTIVE MADNESS. Three women, led by Alexandra Silvia, arrived on the island of Faaite in French Polynesia in August 1987, claiming to be representatives of the Catholic Charismatic Renewal movement, which already had a good following among the island's 180-strong population. The women took over the small church and replaced the lay-preacher as the source of religious authority. Then Silvia, conducting the services in trance, told the islanders that God would abandon Faaite, that demons were in their midst, and that those who failed to attend daily service were open to suspicion. In late August, the three women left the island, having designated seven devoted followers as their disciples. Exorcisms were carried out to rid the devil-possessed, but on 2 September assistant mayor Ioane Harris denounced the movement.

Harris was pronounced possessed, and maddened villagers twisted a cord round his neck, held a crucifix before his face, and beat him senseless. He was then ritually drowned in the lagoon, and his body thrown on a bonfire. Five more people were killed in the next two days. One, a mentally-defective young man who claimed to be Jesus Christ, was burned alive. Another man was strangled and then burned, and his wife hurled alive into the flames. Order was eventually restored on 4 September, a police squad arriving just in time to prevent four further executions. Twenty-four islanders were charged with murder.

CHAPTER FOURTEEN

That Ol' Black Magic

It might be thought that if magic works, the first thing the practitioners would do would be to protect themselves. Alas, tales of invulnerable witches and magicians are few and far between.

THE SMALL VILLAGE OF HESLOUP in Normandy was one of those farming communities where many things had remained unchanged since the Middle Ages: including the tradition of local wizards. Michel Herisson had been using magic since adolescence to cure illnesses and improve the yield of crops and livestock, but the man the villagers really admired was old Jules Camus, whom they thought had far greater supernatural powers than Michel. Surprisingly, on his death-bed in 1973, Jules passed on his powers to Michel, rather than to his own son, Jean. After that, a war of the wizards broke out.

Things started to go wrong for the Herisson family. The barley crop failed and the vineyard dried up, while the cattle developed strange diseases and had to be destroyed. Michel's brother Eugene dropped dead of a heart attack, although he had no previous record of illness. His sister Louisette and a cousin both had road accidents. And when the villagers began to accuse Jean Camus of having the evil eye and causing misery by sticking pins in photographs of his victims, he seems to have accepted the blame, and rejoiced in the title they gave him: The Beast.

The stories had it that Jean had used a curse to kill the village policeman's three small children, and that when the distraught father had tried to shoot the wizard, the bullet had turned back and hit the policeman's own ear. Herisson's elder brother Daniel claimed Jean had predicted he would be killed by a shotgun blast, and shortly afterwards he had wounded himself with his own gun. Obviously Jean was to blame for everything, and no amount of magic seemed to stop him.

Finally, Michel and Daniel decided something had to be done. One night in March 1976 they walked to Jean's tiny cottage and roused him from a drunken stupor. Telling him that he was a more powerful witch doctor, Michel turned Jean's own prediction back on him by blasting him in the head with a shotgun. In the next few days, the sun came out and the crops began to grow again. Michel and Daniel couldn't enjoy the improvement as they were in jail.

TRADITIONAL HEALER Lovemore Mpofu, 40, told his followers in Zimbabwe that his magic powers would allow him to breathe underwater for 48 hours. In September 1990, he organised a tribal cleansing ceremony with a group of 'trainees' at a dam in the south-west of the country, and when he plunged into the water and did not surface, they believed it was part of the rite. For two days the followers danced and sang on the shore, awaiting his return – but by then he had long since drowned.

ZHANG ZHIKE, 25, wanted to become a new emperor of China. Described as a deeply superstitious peasant, Zhike consulted a local sorcerer in the eastern province of Anhui, who told him that his chances were being blocked by a 'fox fairy spirit'. In Chinese tradition, foxes are believed to be able to magically transform themselves into beautiful sexually-vampiric women, and the sorcerer named the spirit as Zhang's new bride, Lu Zhihua. In fact the only strange thing about Lu was that she was a Christian who, worried by her husband's strange behaviour, had summoned people to read the Bible and pray for him. Perhaps they didn't pray hard enough, for in August 1992 Zhang lured his wife to a deserted spot and killed her. His chances of becoming emperor were rather blighted, however, when the police arrested him.

WHEN SHE WAS 17, Madeleine Baumgartner had suffered from excruciating headaches, which doctors had been unable to cure. In desperation her mother went to see Madame Delamare, a "psychic healer" who asked for 100 francs a month, a lock of hair and a photograph, and said she'd call the spirits to help. Amazingly, it worked, and Madeleine got on with her life, marrying a hotel owner in Paris. Then in 1976, Madeleine's mother died, and the headaches returned. By April 1978, 44-year-old Madeleine had worked out that it must be because the payments had stopped, and hired a taxi to take her to Madame Delamare's flat. While the taxi waited outside for 25 minutes, she stabbed the old woman more than a hundred times, then calmly took the taxi back to her husband's hotel. For some reason, she told the driver "I have just killed someone". He believed her, and later informed the police, who tracked down both murderer and victim. Searching Madame Delamare's flat, they found over 200 envelopes, each containing either a photo or a lock of hair, or both, which, at a 100 francs a month each, represented a tidy income. As with the Herissons, Madeleine's life improved: her headaches disappeared and she was feeling much better... but she too ended up in jail.

AFRICA IS RIFE WITH MAGICAL BELIEF. January 1984 saw a rash of witch-burnings and killings in northern South Africa. At the beginning of the month, police arrested 18 villagers at Molethlane after a man and woman had been burned alive, and in the following four weeks seven more people in the Lebowa region were burned at the stake and two hanged. All had been accused of witchcraft, specifically bringing down lightning, and 18 witch doctors were under arrest for the murders. At this time of the year, the area is regularly swept by thunderstorms, and people ask village elders called inyangas to 'sniff out' those who have directed lightning bolts at people and property. By mid-February, 12 had been sacrificed, including a man and two women set alight while tied to a lorry, in Zebediela. Some of the named 'culprits' ran away; others decided to stay and take the punishment, for the simple reason that if they didn't sacrifice themselves, another member of their family would be killed as a substitute.

EVEN MORE GRUESOME events had occurred in Lebowa in November 1978 when former policeman Phuko John Kgabi was arrested with a child's severed windpipe in his pocket. He was captured by the parents of the victim, an eight-year-old girl, when they spotted his car in Seshego township. Kgabi, who became sexually aroused at the sight of blood, was believed to be responsible for the murder of 18 other children in the area, all of whom were mutilated and had had various body parts removed for use in *muti*, the traditional potions and medicines used by witch doctors to promote fertility or cast spells. The previous week, three men had been aquitted of murdering a woman to provide muti for the Prime Minister of Botswana. Kgabi himself was hanged 18 months later.

MOVING TO UGANDA, we find that a rainmaker called Kazaalwa threatened in November 1987 to loose his powers on the village of Rewnyangi unless people showed him more respect and (more importantly, perhaps) a little more generosity. A few days later, hailstorms and high winds lashed the village, ripping the roofs off houses, shops and three schools. Angry villagers immediately decided they knew who was responsible, pushing the rainmaker out into the hailstorm and beating him to death.

IN AUGUST 1989, General Gray Allison was sentenced to death for killing a police private in Liberia. He had used the man's blood in a magic rite to overthrow Liberia's dictator, Samuel Doe.

WICKED INDEED were the deeds of Datu Mangayanon, the 'high priest' of the Ata tribe, who occupied the remote mountain-top village of Gunitan, Mindanao, one of the Philippine Islands. He had promised the villagers that the dried leaves of a tree, which he had ritually killed by hacking it, would turn into money. The tribe waited for days, in September 1985, but the miraculous money failed to appear. Mangayanon sulked, and the villagers muttered. Finally, the magician offered to put things right by inviting the villagers to a feast where they could eat porridge that would "free them from all hardships". Whoever ate some, he said, "would see the image of God". Naïvely, everyone except Mangayanon's wife took his words at face value. The porridge was laced with insecticide, and 68 men, women and children died. There were seven survivors, but they were unable to say whether Mangayanon was among the dead. As for Mangayanon's wife, when she'd refused the porridge, the magician had hacked her to death.

TWO DEACONS of the Pentecostal Church of Jamaica were arrested and sentenced to death in 1978 after the mutilated body of a 22-year-old woman was found in a village four miles from Montego Bay. Her face had been skinned in a religious rite to counteract witchcraft. The local belief is that witches leave their skins behind while they fly through the night.

ROBERT WILLIAMS, 45, CLAIMED to be a witchcraft practitioner, but it didn't seem to do him any good. Having announced his vocation, he lost his job as chief psychologist at the State industrial prison in Hutchinson, Kansas, in 1974. Rather than using magic to get his job back, he shot himself dead.

CHAPTER FIFTEEN

The Ultimate Sacrifice

From magic, we move to more appalling tales. We tend to regard human sacrifice as a practice from the distant past, an act of barbarism no modern person could contemplate. And yet in all parts of the world it still goes on.

FRANÇOIS GODEFRAY OF BIGONVILLE, Luxembourg, was convinced that the people from outer space would be landing soon. The self-styled prophet was well-known to his neighbours as a bit of an eccentric, and that he should start building wooden crates in his garden didn't seem all that remarkable. But when Rosemarie, the 16-year-old daughter of the woman that lived with him, went missing in September 1984, suspicions began to arise. It turned out that Godefray had locked Rosemarie in one of the crates and proceeded to starve her to death as a virgin sacrifice to the alien visitors. "She was pure and untouched by earthly sin," he told police. "I wanted to sacrifice her to the men from another planet who will land soon in a spaceship." The bearded prophet was taken to a mental hospital. No spaceship landings were reported.

CHAPTER FIFTEEN

THE BIBLICAL STORY of Abraham offering his son Isaac as a sacrifice to God is well known to Muslims as well as Jews and Christians. In November 1990 a horrible repeat performance occurred, although this time God failed to send an angel to stop the sacrifice. Ibrahim (Abraham) Halil Altun hacked his three-year-old son to death in a cave after a religious leader he called "my sheikh" told him to sacrifice the most precious thing in his life.

Altun named his instructor as the leader of the Turkish Sunni Muslim Nakshibenbi sect. "My sheikh told me that if one loves his child too much he'll have no love left for God, so I must kill my son," he said. "I took my baby boy Abdullah to a cave and cut him to pieces with a knife. My sheikh said he would bring the child back if I went to a hilltop and shouted Abdullah's name three times. I did so. I did whatever he asked me to do. But my son never came back."

IN MARCH 1984, a 16-year-old boy was beheaded by a Chinese medium in Kuala Lumpur, Malaysia, as a sacrifice for a lucky lottery number. No one at all won the prize that week.

AN UNNAMED FARMER from Sichuan province, west China, had a dream in which he saw his 78-year-old mother standing in front of their home, holding a golden lotus. He thought the dream was a message from on high telling him to sacrifice her in order to obtain good fortune, so he buried her alive.

AND SO TO DECAPITATION MANIA, and a tale which seems completely inexplicable. Iranian Hamid Raza Bayat, 19, was arrested in New York after murdering his father Mahmoud in a bizarre ritual in November 1992. Mahmoud's headless corpse was found in the apartment he shared with his son; he'd also had his middle fingers cut off and his left testicle removed. A cat and a parakeet had also been beheaded, and the heads of five animal statues had been cut off as well. Mahmoud's head, and that of the cat, were found in another part of the building later.

ONE PERSON MURDERING A PARENT is all very well, but when the entire family joins in that seems to be taking things a bit far. Eight members of an Appalachian Mountain family from Inez, Kentucky, were arrested in February 1933 after Lucinda Mills, 72, was sacrificed by her own relatives. Acting on 'Divine commands', her sons, daughters, their spouses and her grandson conducted a rite lasting several hours, which included fasting and speaking in tongues, before her son John strangled her with a chain. The body was placed on a crude altar, but police broke down the barred door of the cabin before the rite could continue. The family members were taken to jail where, apparently lacking all remorse, they continued shouting, praying, chanting and dancing in their cells.

THE MOTIVE IS CLEAR in our next tale, and there's a certain satisfaction in its ending. In Cantagalo, Brazil, police arrested two men, Waldir de Souza and Maria de Conceicao Pontes, in October 1979. They were charged with murdering a two-year-old boy, Antonio Carlos Magalhaes, in a voodoo rite; his blood was then used in a further rite, undertaken in company with their boss and another employee, to magically secure success for a new cement business. In custody, they confessed to five other human sacrifices, but by then a 2,000-strong mob had gathered outside the police station. Before the two men could show police where the victims were buried, they ended up sacrificed themselves, as the mob set fire to police cars, overpowered the guards, beat up the culprits and tossed them into the burning cars.

MORE SYMPATHY IS IN ORDER when desperation drives the deed. A long drought lasted for months in Rhodesia in 1922, and poor crops threatened famine. The elders of the Mtawara tribe held a council and consulted a rainmaker, and decided on a tried and trusted remedy: a human victim publicly burned while the people prayed. They carried out their plan, and 63 people were later charged with murder. Rationally, success was hardly to be expected: but such is the way of things that the drought broke immediately after the sacrifice.

THE VILLAGE OF SIPCHE, near Katmandu in northern Nepal, lost all its men in 1972. The women there believed that if they sacrificed a hundred men, the hundredth would turn into gold and make them rich, while at the same time helping them get to heaven. So they lured all the men in the village to a feast where they served dishes mixed with harital, a poisonous root. All of them died, but no gold appeared: the village was left entirely inhabited by widows and children.

LAXMAN SINGH GIRI was arrested in Bangalore and charged with the murder of three children during the previous five years, and attacks on several others. The 68-year-old sadhu had lived for 27 years at a burial ground in Srirampuram, and it was noticed that the murders took place at full moon. The police conjectured from this that the children were being offered as a blood sacrifice to the goddess

Kali, and kept a watch for unusual activities at the local burial grounds, where such rites are normally conducted. Giri and his accomplices, two men and a woman, were arrested, and the latter confessed all. The sadhu would lurk around playgrounds, selecting his victims and pointing them out to his accomplices; they would then lure the children away with sweets, cut their throats and collect the blood in a bottle. The blood was then used in rites to gain power and immortality.

While he was in custody, there was a total eclipse of the sun on 16 February, 1980 and the sadhu, who had remained silent throughout his interrogation, told his female follower that he had lost his spiritual powers. From that moment on he took no food or sleep and died, still silent, on 5 March apparently of a heart attack.

IN SEPTEMBER 1991, an eight-year-old girl was kidnapped and sacrificed to the gods by villagers near Delhi, India, in a ritual that involved surrounding her body with cloves and chillis, designed to cure another girl of epilepsy. The second girl was believed to be possessed by demons.

IN THE PIROJPUR DISTRICT of Bangladesh, Shahida Khatun murdered her own four-month-old baby in July 1988. She had dreamed that the sacrifice would bring her riches.

OUR CATALOGUE OF HORRORS ends on a more pathetic note. Lolita Arellano, 34, from Bacolod on Negros island in the Philippines, was depressed that the eruption of Mount Pinatubo on Luzon Island had killed 700 people. So at 3am one night in November 1991 she took a scythe and beheaded her three sleeping sons, Manny, 7, Everlito, 6, and

Romulo, 4. She also slit her wrist, but her sister rushed her to hospital and she survived. She told neighbours she was offering her children's heads to pacify the volcano.

CHAPTER SIXTEEN

Cannibalism, Cookery And Blood-Drinking

Like human sacrifice, cases of cannibalism are thought of as buried in the past or practised by primitive tribes, yet they continue today. Strong-stomached readers might care to dine on the following menu, accompanied by a glass or two of blood to wash them down...

WE BEGIN IN HIGH PLACES, with the notorious case of President Idi Amin of Uganda. In 1973 the body of his Foreign Minister Michael Ondanga was found floating in a river with the liver missing. It was found in Amin's headquarters in Kampala, but the president had already eaten part of it. Apparently Amin's Kakwa tribe believed that if part of the victim's liver was eaten, his spirit would not haunt the murderer.

DURING CHINA'S CULTURAL REVOLUTION in the late 1960s, cannibalism was even regarded as an ideologically correct thing to do in the province of Guangxi, where it is claimed that hundreds of political prisoners were killed and eaten by Red Guards. Schoolchildren were encouraged to murder and eat their school principals, and bodies were displayed on meathooks at government cafeterias. When the scandal was eventually uncovered, no one was charged or tried, and less than 100 cannibals were expelled from the Communist Party, some having their pay or rank reduced.

DOCUMENTS DISCOVERED in 1992 showed that more than 100 cases of cannibalism occurred amongst Japanese soldiers abandoned in New Guinea at the close of World War II.

IN THE HAINAN PROVINCE of China Wang Guang was serving a very profitable line in dumplings filled with spicy meat at his White Temple restaurant. They were cheap and delicious and the dumplings, which Wang had been serving since 1987, often sold out. It turned out that Wang's brother Hui, a crematorium worker, had been supplying him with flesh hacked from the thighs and buttocks of corpses. Wang ground up the flesh, mixed it with lots of spices for fear that customers would taste the difference, and billed them as Sichuan-type dumplings. The story only came to light in 1990 when the parents of a young woman killed in a road accident wanted to have a last look at her before cremation, and found that her thighs and buttocks had been removed.

HAO KI WAS A PRISONER released on parole, who began selling mutton kebabs in Harbin, the capital of the northern province of Heilongjiang, China. In February 1993 he strangled a prostitute and cut up her body, then opened her skull and ate her brains, but didn't enjoy the meal much. Two hours later a worker at the kebab stall found the body, so Hao stabbed him to death and later killed and dismembered six other people, including his wife. He also ate the brains of one of these later victims. The 34-year-old was sentenced to death and immediately executed in December 1993.

MACAO, THE PORTUGUESE COLONY on the fringe of China, provides our next ghoulish tale. Here the Cheng family owned a restaurant at the Black Sands tourist resort on the island of Coloane. In June 1985, the entire family of nine, including five children, disappeared along with their servant, and the restaurant was taken over by Wong Chi Hang. Shortly afterwards, 11 severed human limbs (mainly legs and hands) were found washed up on the Black Sands beach.

At first they were thought to have been carried down the Pearl River from China, but police eventually connected them with the Chengs. It transpired that the head of the family, Cheng Lam, had had a long-running argument with Wong over a £12,000 gambling debt; Wong then poisoned the five adults and strangled the children. How he explained to the restaurant staff that he was taking over the business and the family flat isn't known, but Wong then proceeded to cut up the bodies in the kitchen and serve the flesh as 'dim sum' snacks to holiday-makers. He also boiled the skulls of his victims to make soup to serve with the flesh. Wong was eventually arrested in October 1986 as he tried to return to China.

SOME PREFER THEIR SNACKS RAW. A cemetery attendant in the Highfield area of Harare, Zimbabwe, reported coming upon two men and a woman, all naked, devouring the breast and head of an exhumed corpse in October 1992. A crowd gathered outside the cemetery demanding to be allowed to stone the cannibals to death and riot police had to be called.

STRAIGHT OUT OF THE GROUND, too, for a rice-farmer called Wirjo, who hanged himself in April 1987 following a berserk rampage in Wara, at the eastern end of Java. He had been fasting for a month before he snapped, after which he dug up his long-dead mother from the village graveyard and gnawed her bones. Then he took a sickle and hacked to death his son Teuku, 4, and 17 other people, wounding 14 others besides. Apart from the fast, there seemed to be no reason for Wirjo's murder spree.

CANNIBALISM AS REVENGE is perhaps a little more understandable. In October 1987, two men in the Indonesian island of Timor murdered Efraim Bobo, aged 22, for the suspected theft of 27 of their horses. They cut their victim into little pieces, ate parts of his body, and burned the rest to destroy the evidence.

THOSE ALREADY SATIATED on human pork may be relieved as we turn our attention to simple cookery. In Singapore, Ramiah Naragathavally, 33, was arrested in March 1987 along with five members of her family, one of whom was a butcher. They were charged with murdering Naragathavally's husband, a known wife-beater, after which they cut him up and cooked his body in a curry. In this case, however, the curry was simply packed into plastic bags and disposed of in roadside dustbins. Strangely, the family were eventually freed by a Singapore judge, as the prosecution said it had insufficient evidence.

WORKING AS A COOK to start with probably helps in such cases. In New York, kitchen worker Daniel Rakowitz, 28, claimed to be the Antichrist and preached the overthrow of the government; he also murdered his girlfriend, Swiss dancer Monika Beerle, aged 26, in September 1989. Their relationship had gone sour, so he beat and stabbed her to death, then dismembered her in a bathtub and boiled her body in a pot on the kitchen stove.

Where he seems to have gone wrong is that he then left her bones in a bucket in a bus station for the police to find. They were said to be investigating "the possibility that cannibalism occurred", but seemed far more concerned at Rakowitz's expertise in disposing of the body, and reopened their investigations into a number of other murders and disappearances.

FROM EATING TO DRINKING seems a short step, but whether it's a step in the right direction isn't so certain. Lesbian Tracey Wigginton, 25, from Brisbane, Australia, lived as a vampire, avoiding sunlight and mirrors and going out only at night; she lived on pig and goat blood bought from the butchers. Her lover Lisa Ptaschinski would cut her arms so she could drink her blood, and also claimed that Wigginton could read minds and make people disappear, except for their eyes.

In October 1989, Wigginton, Ptaschinski and two other female friends were drinking at a gay club when they decided on a random killing so that Wigginton could drink blood. The four went to Kangaroo Point and posed as prostitutes, where they picked up inebriated roadworker Edward Baldock, 47. They drove him to a deserted yacht club on the Brisbane river where they stripped him to his socks and stabbed him 15 times. Wigginton almost severed his head and drank the blood from Baldock's neck like a shark in a feeding frenzy. After their arrest, Wigginton revealed four separate personalities to psychiatrists under hypnosis. Which one of these was the vampire wasn't clear.

ANOTHER UNCERTAIN PERSONALITY was Alfred John, who was wearing women's clothes when he was arrested by police in Yola, the capital of Nigeria's eastern Adamwa state, in April 1993. The transvestite claimed to have murdered 200 men and women and said he was a 'mammy water', a goddess in a local animist cult. He seems to have been a vampire besides. He told police that he would disguise himself as a woman and, with the aid of water spirits, lure his victims to the banks of the Benue river, where he would kill them and suck their blood.

OUR STRANGEST VAMPIRE TALE features Bahya Lenpeng, 25, who lived in a village in southern Sumatra and had six husbands in two years, killing five of them. On their wedding night, she would give each new husband a sedative, prick one of his arteries and drink his blood while he slept. After a month, the unsuspecting husband would die of anaemia. Her sixth husband, however, was the local police constable, and in June 1975 he only pretended to drink the drugged tea. When Lenpeng decided it was time for some of her own liquid refreshment, he slapped the handcuffs on her and dragged her by the hair to jail. Astonishingly, Lenpeng was given a suspended sentence for manslaughter... and a welcome home from her new husband.

CHAPTER SEVENTEEN

Fatal Food

If eating people is wrong, there also seem to be occasions where eating anything at all can end in disaster. And if we decline a good meal, still there are times when the dinner bites back...

SOUTH AFRICAN Victor Villenti, 50, was a strict vegetarian, and forced his family to follow the same regime. While jogging in 1991 he was killed by an eight-pound frozen leg of lamb which fell from a third storey window.

IN DECEMBER 1993 Alfredo Rosales pegged out from heart and respiratory problems after a monster pig-out in La Plata, 40 miles from Buenos Aires, Argentina. He ate an entire roast sucking pig at one sitting. Fat pig Alfredo weighed 47 stone; the little piggy weighed 26 pounds.

FRANZ WETTSTEIN WAS ONLY 20 when he died in September 1977, but he weighed 49 stone. He was Europe's fattest man. Franz started his working life as a butcher's errand boy, but was sacked when his bicycle collapsed under him. Weighing a mere 30 stone at the time, his next move was into showbusiness. Billed as the 'Eating Machine', he made a meagre living as a sideshow attraction, with customers paying 50p a head to watch him eat. Festival organisers decided he should fatten up a bit, so his daily intake rose to 35 pints of beer, 30 or 40 bread rolls, five pounds of sausages or ten steaks. Under the terms of his contract, he had to keep eating until the last customer went home. Eventually he collapsed with heart trouble. The first ambulance sent to fetch him had to be sent back because it was too small. He survived the attack, but went back to the peepshow afterwards and continued munching... until eventually his heart gave out for the last time. Relatives accused his managers of running off with all the cash he earned... forcing him to eat himself to death.

SNAILS were Marc Quinquadon's particular fancy. The 27-year-old French train driver was already the world record holder for shelling and eating 144 snails in 11 minutes 30 seconds, and was in training for an attempt on 200 when he was guest of honour at a snail dinner in a village near Nancy in November 1979. There he downed 72 snails in three minutes. The next day he collapsed and was rushed to hospital, dying of indigestion shortly afterwards. He weighed 26 stone when he died. His last words were: "I'm not on form."

FOOD MURDERS, next. Not by poisoning, as you might think, but far more direct. Parisian police investigating the death of beautiful Michele Federici in 1976 could see that she had obviously been murdered: there were six stab wounds in her throat and chest. The baffling aspect of the case was that the wounds contained traces of parmesan cheese. Eventually, detective Henri Vantin went to see her husband Othello at his grocery shop and asked him if he stocked parmesan, at which point the shopkeeper broke down in tears and confessed. His wife, 20 years his junior, had spurned his love for months and eventually admitted to an affair with his best friend. Enraged, Othello had grabbed a jagged piece of hard parmesan and stabbed her to death with it. He was found guilty of murder, but released after having spent two years in jail awaiting trial.

A DOUGHNUT was the weapon used by nursing home owner Carol Detlaff, 58, of St Joseph, Michigan, in May 1986. She became upset when Gladys Mulhern, 59, was playing with her food after the other residents had finished, and stuffed the doughnut into her mouth, causing her to choke to death.

MORE RANDOM was the death of Leslie Merry, 56, murdered by a turnip flung from a passing car as he was walking near his home in Leytonstone, east London, in July 1989. He was believed to be the victim of a vegetable-throwing gang responsible for 23 incidents where melons, potatoes and cabbages had been hurled at passers-by. Among the most seriously hurt were a jogger, who needed surgery for internal injuries after being hit in the stomach by a cabbage, and a woman who needed treatment for cuts after her glasses were smashed by a potato. Leslie Merry was struck from behind and at first thought he had been kicked, but saw the turnip rolling away. He was taken to hospital and treated for a fractured rib, but died a few days later from a ruptured spleen. Police failed to find the murder weapon but, explaining how anything could be considered an offensive weapon if a person intends to use it in an assault, remarked that: "If a group of youths are walking or driving around at night with raw turnips or similar vegetables then they are probably not planning to eat them."

COULD FOOD BE MALICIOUS without the intervention of a human hand? A 23-year-old French sweet factory worker was killed by marshmallows in Marseilles in July

1993. A bin filled with 5,000 pounds of soft sweet stickiness tipped up, and he was crushed in the ensuing avalanche.

DEATH WAS SWEET, too, for Joseph LaRose, 31, of Tampa, Florida. He was delivering ice cream to a supermarket in April 1991 when a 500-pound rack of 'Nutty Buddies' fell on him, breaking his leg and crushing his skull.

IN THE MIDST OF FOOD we are in death: in October 1992 California health inspectors carried out a routine check on a fast-food diner in Los Angeles, and found two human corpses in the deep freeze. They were owner Lydia Katash and her lover, who had been strangled at least eight months previously. Astonishingly, no one had found them before the inspection. Police arrested Katash's ex-husband and partner in the business, but the health inspectors were unable to close down the restaurant. If they had found rats or cockroaches, closure would have been instant; but there's nothing in California law to prevent human bodies being stored next to food.

IN BANGKOK, Thailand, a construction worker ate four bags of deep-fried locusts in October 1985. Unfortunately he didn't take into account how the locusts might have been killed, and died shortly afterwards from insecticide poisoning.

SWEET SALESMAN Roland Ohisson of Falkenberg, Sweden, had his last wish granted in October 1993. He was buried in a coffin made entirely of chocolate.

CHAPTER EIGHTEEN

Claws And Paws

We may eat what we like, but is mankind the ruler of the planet? We might like to think so, but the animal kingdom continues to wage its guerrilla war, knocking off a victim here and there.

THE GREATEST SALOON-BAR BORE couldn't invent fish stories as preposterous as this. In June 1811 John Hall, 'a labouring man', went out at low tide to hunt for crabs, at Hume Head near Cawsand. He found a large one among the rocks and tried to pull it out, but the crab caught his hand with its claws and held on so tightly that Hall was unable to either free himself or dislodge the crab. There being no one else around to help him, the tide came in and he was found drowned the following morning.

FISHERMAN Anthony Fernando, 21, died in March 1988 off the coast of Sri Lanka, when a swordfish-like garfish leaped from the water and speared his neck.

A SOUTH KOREAN FISHERMAN was preparing his catch in June 1979, after it had been landed in New Zealand. He thought the tuna he was about to gut was dead, but it flicked its tail, driving the knife he was holding into his chest and killing him.

THE DEATH OF SPANISH ANGLER Maria Cista, 56, had a more direct cause. She was trying to free the hook from a fish's mouth in July 1983 when the fish jumped out of her hand and into her mouth. She choked to death as it wriggled into her throat.

FROM THE VENGEFUL to the opportunistic in our next tale, with an increase in scale besides. In September 1981, an overloaded ferry-boat arrived at Obidos, Brazil, and the 500 passengers crowded to the shore side as it drew up to the dock. The boat capsized, depositing all aboard into a stretch of the Amazon which happened to be a breeding ground for piranhas. As the screaming passengers struggled to reach the shore, shoals of pirhanas ripped into them, attacking again and again in a feeding frenzy which left more than 300 dead, while those who came out of the crimson waters alive suffered horrific bites all over their bodies.

ANOTHER BOATING TRAGEDY, this time in the southern Indian state of Andhra Pradesh, where about 45 guests were returning from a wedding feast across the Godavari River in February 1991. They were travelling in two boats tied together when a water snake slithered into the leading boat. The passengers stampeded to the other side of the boat, which capsized as a result. Twelve people, mostly women and children, were drowned.

MORE SNAKES. Four boys in the western Algerian city of Maghnia, aged from eight to 15, died shortly after eating soup in May 1992. Their mother had inadvertently brought home a poisonous snake hidden among vegetables which she put in the family refrigerator. When she took them out, the snake, seeking warmth, slithered into the soup pot and discharged its venom.

YOUNG GHULAM NABI was mending his motor-scooter in June 1981, on the road from Srinagar, India, to his home 15 miles away. As he crouched there, a kite flew overhead with a live viper in its claws, which it dropped. The snake landed on Nabi's neck and bit him; he died a few minutes later. The kite, however, retrieved the snake and flew off with it.

MAYBE MOTORCYCLISTS are easy targets. Stephen Cawthorne, 43, a former district engineer with the Gas Board, from York, was in the midst of a tour of Australia. On 23 July 1993 he died from head injuries when his Yamaha 600cc motorcycle collided with a young emu which jumped from a grassy bank into his path. This unexpected event occurred when he had just overtaken a caravan on a narrow cutting near Mount Surprise, Queensland, and there was no room for manoeuvre when the three-foot-tall emu sudddenly appeared. A cloud of feathers filled the air as he hit the bird at 50mph, then Cawthorne somersaulted over the handlebars and died instantly from head injuries and a broken neck. The emu, a bird noted for its stupidity and its tendency to run towards loud noises, was also killed.

SALIMU HATIBU, 27, was convicted in December 1990 of stealing from a church in north-eastern Tanzania. He fled the court and plunged into a river where, in what looks like a case of divine vengeance, he was eaten by a crocodile. His body was never recovered.

CHAPTER EIGHTEEN

FROM DIRECT ATTACKS, we move to use of weapons. In Venice, Georgio Scrimmin, 55, was kept awake by a howling cat in October 1992. He leaned out of his bedroom window and tried to hit it with a broom. The terrified cat leapt over his head onto the roof, where it dislodged a slab of marble which fell onto Scrimmin's head and killed him.

IN MONTANA a driver lost control of his lorry in August 1979 when a fly flew into his mouth and bringing on a choking fit. The lorry crashed, killing his wife who was in the cab with him.

CANOEIST Nanette Meech, 76, of Santa Fe, California, was making her way down the Brule River in Wisconsin with her daughter Laurie on 15 July 1993. On the nearby bank stood a 40-foot poplar tree, about 18 inches in diameter, which had been gnawed by a beaver. As they passed, it crashed down, striking Mrs Meech on the head and killing her.

DOGS THAT SHOOT THEIR OWNERS are a well-chronicled phenomenon. Here's a particularly choice example of the genre. In Bingen, Germany, Eric Dankert faced a murder charge in January 1982, when his wife Maria, 31, was shot dead with a rifle as she played the piano. But Dankert, 64, explained that Maria had asked him to show her how the gun worked, as she was nervous when left alone in the house. As he held the gun, his pet alsatian Dixie jumped up at him and pulled the trigger with his paw, shooting Maria dead. When Dixie and the gun were taken into a field and it was shown that he could set off the gun, Dankert was freed... but Dixie died soon afterwards when he accidentally ate rat poison.

THE CASE OF IRANIAN HUNTER Ali-Ashgar Ahani is an interesting variation on the theme. In April 1990 the 27-year-old tried to catch a snake alive near Teheran by pressing the butt of his shotgun behind its head. The snake coiled round the butt and pulled the trigger with its thrashing tail, firing one of the barrels and shooting Ahani fatally in the head. As his colleague tried to grab the shotgun, the writhing reptile triggered the other barrel, but this shot seems to have missed.

FROM THE SMALL TO THE LARGE, and a tale to show the futility of arguing with an elephant – let alone an entire herd. In November 1984 a herd of wild elephants destroyed large areas of rice and banana crops in Syamtalira Bayu in Sumatra. They were led by a large white bull elephant and damaged 14 villages besides. A villager called Hussein tried to defend his crops by grabbing hold of the trunk of the charging white bull and slashing out with a knife. The elephant hurled him 10 feet into the air and, when he landed, the whole herd of 36 elephants trampled him to death.

BARKING doesn't just irritate humans, it seems. In February 1993, 50-year-old Heibrecht Beukes from Pretoria was walking her pooch in the Mabelingwe nature reserve in Transvaal, South Africa. Upset by the dog's barking, an enraged hippopotamus smashed its way through an electrified fence, apparently oblivious to the shocks, and trampled and bit Beukes to death. The hippo was later shot.

A COBRA was raised by a woman from Trincomalee, Sri Lanka, in the belief that the snake was a reincarnation of her dead son. In July 1984, she died when the snake bit her.

CHAPTER EIGHTEEN

A PET MONKEY in Malaysia became enraged in January 1978 at his master's insistence that he should take a daily swim. The primate turned on the man and bit him to death. Neighbours killed the animal with sticks.

A COW that had been bought for sacrifice at a Moslem religious festival in Pakistan may have realised the fate that was in store for it. In September 1984 it went berserk and killed its 60-year-old owner.

CHAPTER NINETEEN

Rotten Shots

Guns, of course, are dangerous weapons, but so are many other things, particularly in the hands of the less than competent. Whether it be lousy aim, accidental misidentification or downright stupidity, the results are all too often fatal...

HUNTERS mistaking a colleague for their prey and blasting them to death are so numerous that one wonders occasionally whether all of them might not be variants on a single contemporary legend.

In November 1990 Charles Boyer, 43, went turkey-hunting in Deerfield Township, Pennsylvania. In order to get near the birds, he daubed his clothes with blue and grey patches to look like turkey heads, crouched behind a bush and made gobbling sounds. Ninety yards away, Troy Moore heard him, spotted something moving, and shot Boyer dead.

YUGOSLAVIAN IMPRESSIONIST Dragutin Ilic went off to the woods in October 1978 to practice his rutting stag imitation. So lifelike was Dragutin's mimicry that he was shot and killed by a poacher.

CHAPTER NINETEEN

A JAPANESE HOUSEWIFE from Hyogo, near Osaka, was gathering bamboo for New Year decorations in December 1993 when the 52-year-old was shot dead by a hunter who mistook her for a deer.

A NEW ZEALAND FARMER was hunting rabbits with his 10-year-old son in November 1988. They were trying to flush out rabbits from their farmhouse when the boy fell through a trapdoor in the floor and began crawling about between the house piles. Noticing the movement, the farmer fired his rifle, hitting his son in the forehead and killing him.

MOST PECULIAR OF ALL was the case of Robert Duncan, of Aberdeen, Washington. In December 1991 he was killed by either Richard Dailey or Richard Tupper, who were out hunting grouse. Duncan was sitting in his daughter's kitchen drinking coffee at the time.

A MOTORIST IN NORTHERN NAMIBIA in August 1989 ran over a porcupine, stopped the car, and decided to put the injured animal out of its misery by clubbing it to death with his shotgun. In doing so, he managed to shoot himself dead. What happened to the porcupine was never established.

TIME FOR A TALE of downright stupidity. In November 1991, Clarence Lewis, 49, was at home babysitting his grandchildren in LaPlace, Louisiana. He got so fed up with watching children's programmes on the television that he pulled out a .45 pistol from under the cushion of his armchair and decided he was going to shoot out the screen. His aim being less than perfect, Lewis missed the television set entirely and shot his wife Sara straight through the head, killing her instantly.

SOME STORIES are ready-scripted arguments for gun control. In Wilmington, California, an unnamed teenager boasted to his friends about his .38 calibre revolver, in March 1992. Showing off, he fired four or five bullets into the air. One of them hurtled down out of the sky half a mile away and hit five-year-old Adrian Benitez in the head as he was walking with his mother and brother. Adrian died six days later when he was taken off a life support machine. The teenager was tracked down and arrested.

AT AN APARTMENT COMPLEX in the north-east of Austin, Texas, William Howard Tate, 43, picked up his .45 calibre semi-automatic in June 1988, without realising it was loaded. Fortunately for him, he was pointing it at the floor when it went off. Less fortunate was the unnamed man lying in bed in the apartment below: the bullet went straight through the floor and hit him in the chest. He was pronounced dead at the scene.

ROMOLO RIBOLLA, 42, wanted to blow his head off. In April 1981 he sat in the kitchen of his home near Pisa, Italy, gun in hand and threatening to kill himself. He was depressed because he couldn't find a job. For nearly an hour his wife Emilia pleaded with him not to do the deed. Finally he burst into tears and threw the gun to the floor. It went off and killed his wife.

YOU CAN ALMOST SEE the end coming in our next story; sadly Nicholas Lovell couldn't. In December 1987, the 16-year-old student was working on a computer at the home of his friend David Duquette, 19, in Gloucester, Rhode Island. Lovell began to hiccup, at which point Duquette decided that the best way to cure him was to give him a fright. He went to his parents' room and got a .38 calibre revolver, which he assumed was unloaded. Placing the gun to the back of Lovell's head, he shouted "Bang!" The gun was loaded, curing Lovell of his hiccups with extreme prejudice.

VILLAGE POLICEMAN Marc Fagny, 48, from Arlon in Belgium, was sent to shoot a rabid alsatian in October 1991... and killed the woman who owned the dog instead. At his trial for manslaughter, he said that everybody in the village knew that he couldn't shoot straight.

FABIO SPANU TRIED TO KILL a turkey for dinner on his farm in Nuoro, Sardinia, in February 1992. The 20-year-old swung his axe, missed the bird, and hit himself in the chest. He died on the way to hospital. As a police spokesman remarked: "He was not very expert in killing turkeys."

POLISH TRUMPETER Krysztof Baschuz, 24, played in the orchestra of a travelling circus which arrived in Aubena, France, in August 1982. Also amongst the circus crew was crossbow-man Tony Bertolazzi, 22, who specialised in bursting balloons. Missing the target, Bertolazzi's bolt hit the trumpeter in the eye and killed him.

A SCHOOLTEACHER IN THAILAND used a real pistol to start races at the school sports day in November 1993. As he waved youngsters back after a false start, the gun went off and killed a six-year-old boy.

CHAPTER TWENTY

Mysteries And Murders

After relating so many odd but understandable deaths, it's time for a collection of some of the more peculiar tales in our files: the weird, the unexplained, the stories that seem to come direct from a mystery-writer's casebook...

HEATING ENGINEER Roy Orsini of North Little Rock, Arkansas, was planning to leave home at 4.30 one morning in March 1981 to drive to a distant business appointment. Orsini went to bed at 9pm and, as usual when he was to get up early, his wife Lee slept with their 13-year-old daughter Tiffany so she wouldn't be disturbed. Next morning after breakfast, Lee walked Tiffany to school and then returned home and began doing the housework. Finishing the downstairs rooms, she went upstairs and found the bedroom door locked from the inside. Orsini had never locked the bedroom door before and when there was no response to her calls Lee checked the garage, finding her husband's car still there. Worried, Lee went for help to her neighbour, Glenda Walker, who brought a hammer and screwdriver, with which they broke open the door.

Orsini, still in his pyjamas, lay face down on the bed with a .38 calibre bullet in his head. Suicide was ruled out, because although Orsini owned a .38 pistol, it was in a chest of drawers several feet from the bed. Obviously, no one shoots themselves in the head, puts the gun away and then returns to lie down on the bed. Besides, tests showed that Orsini had not handled a gun before his death, and his gun was a Smith & Wesson, while the bullet that killed him had come from a Colt. It was undoubtedly murder, apparently carried out between midnight and 1am. Yet no one had heard a shot, suggesting that the murder was carried out with a silencer, and so probably premeditated. Police could find no motive or past enemies. There were no fingerprints apart from those of the family. Nothing was missing, and there were no signs of forced entry. More curious still, the windows were locked from the inside as well as the door, so there seems no way the murderer could have escaped.

THE DEATH OF BELINDA BURNETT in December 1992 baffled police in Keansburg, New Jersey. Her body was found in a closet at a house frequented by drug users, and she had been hit in the face and strangled. Weirdly, she had been stripped half naked and covered in white paint.

ANOTHER LOCKED ROOM MURDER case came from northern France in August 1966. Bachelor Anton Przewozny, 59, was found beaten to death in his room on a farm at d'Avrainville Essonne. Other workers had heard his cries for help and banged on the locked door of his room. When his cries stopped they called the police. They found the shotgun used as a bludgeon back in its proper place, but the door had been locked from the inside and the window bolted. There was soft soil below the 17-foot-high window, but no footprints. And inside the room was another puzzle: there was an ashtray full of cigarette ends, but Przewozny did not smoke.

FROM MARSEILLES comes a tale with all the trimmings. In May 1966, Emile Hervé, 47, was taken ill at his home in the Rue Camille Flammarion in the French seaport. Police inspector Jean Darian drove a doctor to the house, but when they arrived a power failure plunged the place into darkness. They were taken upstairs to the sick room by a member of the family with candles, and they left the door open for more light as the doctor examined his patient. They were too late; Hervé had just died. Then the door slammed shut, blowing out the candles, and a gunshot rang out. Almost immediately the door was opened as the family rushed to find out what had happened. The doctor was face down over his dead patient, also dead with blood oozing from a gunshot wound in his back, and on the floor by the inspector was a .22 rifle.

Detectives were called, as well as an examining magistrate who ordered an immediate reconstruction of the scene. The dead men were left on the bed, the same candles were lit, the door was opened and the rifle, which had already been fingerprinted, was stood back against the wall in its original position. The windows were found to be closed from the inside, there was no sign of an intruder, and all the circumstantial evidence pointed toward Darian. They went through the reconstruction several times, with the inspector protesting his innocence, but it was only near dawn that he was cleared – as he had been implicated – by an accident. A gust of wind blew the door shut, blowing out the candles and knocking down the rifle, which was found with its muzzle pointing toward the bed.

CHAPTER TWENTY

NO MURDER MYSTERY IS COMPLETE without its element of judicial puzzlement. Everyone in the little Syrian village of Kamsihly knew about Abbas Ahmand and his wife Zehra. There were regular noisy quarrels, and Zehra would sometimes turn up at the marketplace with bruises or a black eye. When Abbas himself went to market one day, no one was surprised at his explanation: he told them Zehra had decided she couldn't live with him any more, and had left him and the children. But next morning a farmer found the decapitated body of a woman in his cornfield. Some of the villagers identified the body as Zehra and, with their past record of domestic quarrels, the police arrested Abbas. His protests were not believed, and he was sentenced to life imprisonment. Five years later, in August 1980, Zehra returned to Kamsihly, now 30 years old and unaware that she was officially dead. She explained that she really had left and got a job in the city, but she missed her children and wanted to see them and Abbas. She was reunited with her kids, who had been raised by relatives, and Abbas was pardoned and released. He went straight home and strangled his wife in front of the children. He told police: "I don't believe that she didn't know I was in jail. She had to pay for my five lost years." Abbas was promptly returned to jail, leaving Syrian lawyers to ponder whether a man can be tried twice for the same murder – even though he was convicted before he committed it.

AN UNIDENTIFIED MAN was found dead on Dartmoor in March 1975, but forensic tests failed to show a cause of death, so police were unable to say whether he met his end as a result of murder, suicide or natural causes. He was wearing a normal suit and ordinary shoes, quite unsuitable for the moor. He was carrying a detailed ordnance survey map of the area and had a small amount of cash, but nothing that would identify him. Also in his pockets were 12 hard-to-obtain cyanide capsules containing enough poison to kill 30 people and a bottle of poisonous laburnum seeds, but there was no trace of either poison in his body. Perhaps most baffling of all was the last item he carried with him: a bottle of sweet and sour sauce.

MORE PUZZLING STILL is the tale of Gerald Marten, with its strange and supernatural overtones. The 26-year-old chef was found dead in his car in the garage of his mother's home at Braintree, Essex, in August 1981. His mother had been on holiday and he had been dead for eight days when he was discovered. It seemed an open and shut case, but police stopped the funeral just as the cortege arrived at the crematorium and demanded the body be taken away for further identification tests. It turned out that Marten was indeed the dead man but an unnamed yet "respectable and responsible" couple who had known him for three years had approached the police and claimed to have met him in Braintree's Market Square after he was dead. Police said: "They cannot be dissuaded from the fact that they saw, spoke to and even shook hands with the person they knew as Gerald Marten two hours after he was found dead and more than a week after he is believed to have died." There seemed to be no explanation, but the spokesman continued: "We do not doubt that the couple are telling the truth."

FROM THINGS WE CANNOT KNOW to things we probably don't want to be involved with. Howard Green, 53, and his girlfriend Carol Mannon, 33, had lived together for seven years in Brooklyn, New York. He was a cab driver and abstract painter, while she was a secretary who wrote poetry and occasionally sold one-off dresses. During the last weeks of their lives they were said by friends to be delving deeply into occult practices, but what kind wasn't clear. They were both found dead on 15 December 1979 off Route 80 in West Patterson, New Jersey. They were wrapped in a carpet, and had identical injuries: their heads were bludgeoned on the left side, each had a right eye wound and similar cuts and bruises about knees and groin. Both clutched clumps of hair in each fist, which police said was a symbol used by some satanic groups. And each had been completely drained of blood, leaving so little that there was insufficient to take lab samples.

There are further strange twists to the tale. Two weeks before her death, Mannon told a friend she was writing a story in which the Shah of Iran was kidnapped, tortured and hung so that the blood drained from his body. The couple also had a one-time neighbour who captured mice and drained their blood, but at the time of the murder the man seemed to be in Oklahoma... at about the same time that several cows were found dead with their blood drained. Police were baffled. "Right now," said the detective in charge, "I'm looking for 15 pints of blood."

JAMES BURNS, 40, of Houston, Texas, was paralysed below the neck after a former wife shot him in the spine in 1979. In August 1987 he married again, but two weeks later he thought new wife Berta, 37, was cheating on him. As he sat in his wheelchair, he persuaded her to put a piece of string in his mouth. At the other end of the string was a pistol in a container on his lap. He jerked his head back and pumped three rounds into her, shooting her dead.

CHAPTER TWENTY-ONE

Funeral Follies

We conclude with tales from the funeral parlour, the final rites and the burying ground. And here we find that the end of life for one is also the beginning of death for others.

AT THANJAVUR, in the southern Indian province of Tamil Nadu, a Hindu priest was officiating at a funeral in January 1991. In Hindu belief, Yama the god of death rides on a water buffalo whenever he rises up from hell to pluck away a dying person's soul. So it was more than a little appropriate when the priest was suddenly set upon and gored to death by a water buffalo, maddened by the bite of a rabid dog. The buffalo was later captured and killed by vets, but by then the god of death had doubled his tally for the day.

A MOSLEM FUNERAL in the Kashmiri capital of Srinagar was the scene of mass accidental death in May 1992. Virtually all of the 90 dead were women, who, according to custom, do not sit with men on public occasions. Two hundred women were gathered on the top floor of the house of Mirza Ghulam Mohammad, whose daughter Naseema had died of a brain haemorrhage, when the wooden floorboards collapsed under their weight. They fell through onto 100 more women on the floor below, and then bodies and wreckage crashed through to the ground floor. Apart from the 81 killed on the spot, including Naseema's mother, 100 were injured; and some of these died later in hospital from suffocation, when mobs crammed the wards.

A DISPUTE BROKE OUT in September 1986 between two brothers-in-law in Vallefiorita, Italy, about who was entitled to the last free space in the family tomb. Things soon became so heated that one man stabbed the other to death and, on a first-come first-served basis, did himself out of the vacancy.

A DISTINCTLY GRISLY TALE comes from Gaenheim, in southern Germany. A 91-year-old woman was certified dead from heart failure and buried in January 1986. After the mourners left, gravedigger Emil Graf was shovelling the earth back in to the grave when he heard a knocking as if the old woman was kicking the coffin lid. He fetched five people from the funeral firm responsible for the ceremony, and for 10 minutes they stood around listening as the sounds grew fainter and stopped. Then they carried on and filled in the grave.

WE NOW COME to a tale which has passed into legend, oft-repeated in various forms. Who knows if or when the events really happened, but this is the earliest version in our files, from February 1980. In Bujumbura, Burundi, a man bought a coffin in which to bury a relative and loaded it onto his open-backed lorry. Somewhere along the road, the co-driver slipped into the coffin for a nap and, as the rain started to pour down, closed the lid. Without him knowing it, the driver picked up five hitch-hikers, who took their place on the back of the truck; and they, in turn, thought they were riding with an empty coffin. Eventually the co-driver woke up and removed the coffin lid, causing panic among the hitch-hikers, all five of whom leapt off the speeding lorry to their deaths.

UNDERTAKER'S ASSISTANT Jack Volkering, 59, picked up an encoffined body from a memorial mass in February 1989 and drove it away in his hearse to prepare it for the actual funeral. As he drove along Highway 27 in Cold Spring, Kentucky, a car driven by 23-year-old Lonnie Stephens crossed the road and hit the hearse head-on. Stephens received only minor injuries, but the impact caused the coffin and its contents, weighing 22 stone, to hurtle forwards. It broke through a metal holding post and smashed into Volkering's back, crushing him to death against the steering wheel and dashboard.

ARRIVING AT THE SERVICE ITSELF, we have mourners, preacher and pall-bearers gathered together; and in the following tales death gathers in one of each for a complete set. Fred Dumelow, 71, attended the funeral in January 1991 of his life-long friend Albert Decamps, 75. Unfortunately, after the service began at St George's church in Ticknell, Derbyshire, Fred slumped in his pew and died. His body then became wedged between his seat and the one in front, and all efforts to free it failed. After discussions between the Reverend Norman Lifton and the mourners, it was decided to cover Fred's body with a sheet, and carry on with the service as normal. As Lifton explained: "The trouble was that we had to be at the crematorium on time. If one funeral is late all the others are held up. The undertakers were getting agitated." Time and the crematorium schedule, it seems, wait for no man.

THE FUNERAL of businessman William Douch, 52, took place in a tiny Welsh chapel at Brechfa, Dyfed, in December

1989. All was going well as Reverend Haydn Richards, 57, took his place in the pulpit and began reading the lesson. Halfway through, Richards collapsed and, though the mourners rushed to help him, also died of a heart attack. Everyone was too upset to carry on, so the funeral was abandoned.

SURVIVING THE SERVICE may not be the end of the problem. In March 1980, when the funeral cortège arrived at the cemetery in Gileston, near Cardiff, they found the grave already occupied. Gravedigger Percy Overton, 54, had suddenly collapsed and died, falling into the grave he had just prepared for pensioner Jim Barnes. The service was delayed for 45 minutes while his body was removed.

DEATH LISTENS IN to our every word, it seems. In July 1982 the Reverend Ray Hewett had just concluded the burial of Liza Poteete, 91, in Blairsville, Georgia, with the words "we never know who's going next" when a bolt of lightning struck dead her 27-year-old grandson, Donald Metcalf.

TWO UNDERTAKERS SHOT EACH OTHER dead in Paraiba, north-eastern Brazil, during an argument over who had the right to conduct the funeral of one of the town's inhabitants. Another undertaker from a neighbouring town was called in to bury all three bodies.

References

REFERENCES

INSIDE FRONT COVER

Fowl Death: La Provincia (Spain), 11 Dec 1990.

CHAPTER 1: CUPID'S DEADLY DARTS

Ferrozzo: D. Mail, D. Mirror, 25 Nov 1983. *Daniels*: Times-Reporter (Ohio), 22 Jan, D. Express, 23 Jan 1988. *Hidaka*: D.Mirror, 11 Oct 1992. *Min Chou Lin*: Celebrity, 19 Nov 1987. *Dunja*: News of the World, 15 June 1980. *Keoghoe* Sussex Evening Argus, 3 Dec 1993. *Farrand*: Weekend, 19 July 1978. *Paler*: News on Sunday, 8 Nov 1987. *Cantori*: Dracula (Romania), 1 June 1993. *Momescu*: Weekend, 12 July 1978. *Kneen*: D. Telegraph, 8 April 1993. *Nelson*: D. Record, 22 Mar 1993. *Turkish roof-falls*: Guardian, 16 Nov 1990. *Orionno*: D. Mirror, 24 Oct 1988. *Newman*: D. Telegraph, 14 July 1992. *Brayboy*: Independent, 7 Dec 1990. *Vela*: Middlesbrough Evening News, 27 June 1987.

CHAPTER 2: THE FONT AND THE ALTAR

Guy: Western Morning News, 21 June 1993. *N. Carolina couple*: Guardian, 8 June 1987 *Pakistan wedding*: D. Record, 15 March 1993. *Mathai*: S. Express, 10 July 1977. *Yang Baosheng*: Xinmin Evening News, 11 June 1991. *Cundiff*: D. Mail, 26 June 1979. *Jordanian wedding*: Guardian, 1 Oct 1990. *Blue*: E. Standard, 7 Sept 1983. *Hoffmann*: D. Record, 21 Oct 1991. *Weltz*: People, 12 Sept 1993. *Zhang*: E. Standard, 18 Feb 1992.

CHAPTER 3: MORE THAN ANYONE CAN STAND

Huang Yashuo: South China Morning Post, 9 Feb 1993. *Allen*: Pawtuxet Valley Daily Times, 12 July 1986. *Love*: S. Mail, 20 Oct 1991. *Losier*: N.Y. Times, 21 March 1988. *Mancuso*: S. Express, 18 Nov 1990. *Taylor*: D. Telegraph, 9 March 1991. *Fowler*: AP wire, ? July 1989. *D'alessio*: News of the World, 28 Feb 1993. *Dominguez*: D. Star, 27 Nov 1992 *Corlett*: D. Telegraph, 9 + 10 + 15 July 1987. *Fallar*: AP wire, 17 Aug 1992. *Jeurgens*: S. Mail, 9 Sept 1990. *Guy*: D. Telegraph, 23 July 1988. *Hicks*: The Scotsman, 10 Dec 1986. *St. Marcel schoolboy*: Reveille, 24 March 1978. *Casanova*: Weekend, 31 May 1978. *Krefeld professor*: E. Standard, 6 May 1988. *Mori*: Sun, 3 July 1986. *Vizonis*: D. Telegraph, 18 Mar 1985. *Lumia*: Sun, 25 March 1993. *Miami boy*: Sussex Evening Argus, 18 Sept 1993. *Sun Taichang*: Guardian, 17 Oct 1987. *Dong Huibo*: D. Record, 15 Aug 1992.

REFERENCES

CHAPTER 4: A RIDICULOUS WAY TO GO

Mitchell: Times, 29 March 1975. *Johnson*: D. Telegraph, 28 Oct 1992. *Sanchez*: D. Star, 7 Jan 1993. *Lecuere*: Celebrity, 30 June 1988. *Pitioret*: D. Record, 24 March 1993. *Townsend*: North Devon Journal-Herald, 22 April 1982. *Santos + Ja*: The Orcadian, 11 June 1987. *Philippines beauty argument*: D. Telegraph, 13 June 1987. *Whisner*: Southland Times, 25 July 1989. *Hommel*: People, 10 Oct 1993. *Grundman*: D. Mail, 17 Aug 1990. *Hamm*: Victoria Times-Colonist, 29 Jan 1989. *Ray*: D. Telegraph, 16 Sept 1988. *Alicante con-man*: Johannesburg Citizen, 16 May 1991. *Barrera*: Europa Times, Jan 1994. *Jules*: D. Record, 2 Jan 1992. *Singh*: D. Mirror, 20 Nov 1992. *Austin man*: Reuters wire, 11 May 1983. *LeDoc*: S. Mail, 20 June 1993. *Brooklyn Bridge man*: D. Mirror, 18 May 1993. *Commerce man*: Independent, 4 March 1988. *Sharma*: D. Star, 10 Jan 1994. *Chinese soldiers*: Guardian, 13 June 1984.

CHAPTER 5: SNOW JOBS

Bowers: Shropshire Star, 16 Jan, D. Express, 17 Jan 1980. *Morrell*: D. Mail, D. Express, 1 Mar 1989. *Gados*: Unidentified (US) newspaper, 30 Dec 1988. *German Pilots*: Sun, 12 Mar 1984. *Winter*: D. Mirror, 10 Jan 1984. *Smalls*: D. Telegraph, 22 Jan 1981. *Landis*: Sun, 20 Nov 1982. *Sanchez*: D. Express, 11 Oct, Independent, 12 Oct 1990. *Heer*: D. Telegraph, 10 Jan 1986. *Rutelli*: D. Record, 28 Feb 1991. *Reader*: D. Post, D. Telegraph, 27 April 1990.

CHAPTER 6: REVENGE OF THE MACHINES

Niskala: Victoria Times-Colonist, 18 Sept 1987. *Chester sawmill*: Shropshire Star, 22 Nov 1983. *Gooch*: D. Mirror, 20 April 1988, The Record (NJ), 5 April 1988. *Davis*: D. Mirror, 22 April 1991. *Russell*: News of the World, 23 Feb 1975 *Rodriguez*: Atlanta Journal & Constitution, 4 Dec 1988. *Thomas*: Boston Globe, 13 Aug 1987. *Maguire*: S. Press, 10 Jan 1993. *Kenyon*: D. Mirror, 26 May 1988. *Charters*: D. Telegraph, 10 Nov 1983. *Mitchell*: Washington Times, 29 March 1993. *Prado*: N.Y. Daily News, 12 May 1992. *Urada*: D. Mirror, 17 May 1993. *Magnasco*: Sun, 23 Aug 1993. *Gudkov*: Sun, 5 March 1992. *Castro*: D. Star, 9 Jan 1991. *Aierguma*: Independent, 30 July 1991.

CHAPTER 7: THE LONG ARM OF COINCIDENCE

New Orleans lifeguards: Sun, 16 April 1992. *Doucette*: Augusta Chronicle, 25 Feb 1990. *Parker*: D. Telegraph, 9 Jan 1987. *Collier*: Birmingham Evening Mail, 8 Dec 1971. *Cave*: D. Post, 18 June 1982. *Smoke*: Bay City Times Press, 13 Aug 1901. *Squelch*: D. Telegraph, 13 Aug 1987. *Alton*: Western Morning News, 30 March 1987. *Kolominn + Gessner*: E. Standard, 19 April 1988. *Ebbin*: Liverpool Echo, 21 July 1975. *Akgun*: Hurriyet, 29 Sept 1991. *Slabbert*: D. Mirror, 13 Oct 1987. *Richardson + Bradbury*: Urmston & Stretford Journal, 16 Jan 1974. *Graziano*: S. Express, 7 Oct 1984. *Orr*: Manchester Evening News, 8 Oct 1991. *French avalanche*: D. Mirror, 29 Dec 1980. *Stewart*: North West Arkansas Times, 7 April 1983.

REFERENCES

CHAPTER 8: DEATH CHAINS

Menominee: Dominion (N.Z.), 31 July 1989. *Rawalpindi*: Weekly News, 21 April 1979. *Buenos Aires*: Nairobi Standard, 24 Oct 1988. *Porto Vesme*: D. Telegraph, 7 Aug 1993. *Limani*: D. Telegraph, 17 Aug 1984. *Tarbet*: D. Telegraph, 16 June 1993. *Gibson Co.*: St. Catherine's Journal, 30 May 1839. *Zabolotye*: Guardian, 21 June 1988. *Angthong*: Johannesburg Citizen, 30 April 1991. *Woodseaves*: Sun, 16 Nov 1990. *Craven family*: D. Telegraph, 31 Aug, D. Mirror, 1 + 4 Sept 1990. *Budapest*: Weekend, 12 Aug 1981.

CHAPTER 9: SECOND TIME AROUND

Zarif: Independent, 7 + 8 Oct 1992. *Brentwood woman*: Sun, 14 Sept 1990. *Millbank*: Independent, 23 Jan 1993. *Luise*: S. Express, 13 Feb 1983. *Kreekmore*: S. Express, 3 Feb 1985. *Gregorio*: Victoria Times-Colonist, 15 Feb 1989. *Quinanola*: Houston Post, 13 Sept 1990. *Schwartz*: S. Express, 11 Dec 1983. *Bombay women*: AP wire, etc, 14 Oct 1993. *Rio Negro man*: D. Telegraph, 12 Aug 1977. *Chan Wai-fong*: Independent, 12 July 1991. *Philippou*: D. Telegraph, 27 Jan 1990.

CHAPTER 10: THEY BROUGHT IT ON THEMSELVES

Sharland: D. Telegraph, 18 Aug 1989. *Stewart*: D. Star, 14 Jan 1992. *Symanski*: Guardian, 27 April 1993.*Grahamstown man*: N.Y. Post, 2 Jan 1992. *Sutherland*: San Jose Mercury News, 20 June 1993. *Ito*: Sun, 26 Sept 1979. *Oki*: S. Express, 4 Aug 1985. *Reynolds*: Weekly News, 23 June 1979. *Davidovitch*: D. Mirror, 16 Dec 1976. *Butterick*: Vancouver Sun, 11 March 1980. *Ramos*: Guardian, 26 Oct 1983. *Newt man*: Beaumont Enterprise & Journal, 11 Aug 1981. *Hallas*: Guardian, D. Telegraph, 18 Dec 1979. *Tyree*: Cincinnati Enquirer, 2 Oct 1988. *Montpol*: S. Express, 6 Oct 1985. *Gleffe*: E. Standard, 29 May 1979. *New York man*: New Sunday Times, 10 July 1977.

CHAPTER 11: BY THEIR OWN HAND

Cheung Yuen-Man: South China Morning Post, 6 Aug 1992. *Rankin + Collins*: S. People, 18 July 1976. *Killington*: D. Mirror, 24 April 1981. *Bennett*: D. Mirror, 26 Sept 1991. *Frankenstein*: News-Sun (Illinois) 11 March 1981. *Fong Yee Pin*: Guardian, 2 Oct 1990. *Versturme*: D. Telegraph, 23 Jan 1988. *Williamson*: D. Star, 6 April 1993. *Allanson*: D. Mirror, 30 April 1985. *Boothroyd*: Independent, 11 June 1987. *Daley*: D. Telegraph, 11 Nov 1993. *Brun*: Victoria Times-Colonist, 1 Sept 1987. *Robins*: D. Post, 6 Sept 1988. *Chinese peasant girls*: Evening Post (N.Z.), 17 Oct 1988. *Chinese pensioners*: South China Morning Post, 21 May 1993. *East London cliff-death*: Weekly News, 15 Dec 1979.

CHAPTER 12: IT'S THE VOICES

Greco: Victoria Times-Colonist, 25 Feb 1989. *Gonzales*: Houston Chronicle, 16 Feb 1981. *Donaldson*: Toronto Sun, 31 March 1993. *Dowdeswell*: D. Telegraph, 19 May 1979. *Racnil*: Guardian, 19 June 1986. *Trofimov*: Cleveland Plain Dealer, 3 Nov 1988. *Swindon*: Middlesbrough Evening Gazette, 16 Dec 1989. *Triplett:* Edinburgh Evening News, 24 Jan 1991. *Vernicci*: News on Sunday, 8 Aug 1987.

REFERENCES

CHAPTER 13: THE MADNESS OF CULTS

Haigler: D. Express, 5 July 1982. *Maneja*: Guardian, 12 Aug 1985. *Sun Yingpeng*: Saudi Gazette, 12 May 1987. *Ca Van Liem*: E. Standard, 12 Oct 1993. *Kumbakonam bathers*: Guardian, 19 Feb 1992. *Khadeshwari Baba*: Times of India, 5 Nov 1980. *Tanzanian Pathfinders*: San Francisco Chronicle, 29 Nov 1993. *Maurice + Piersotte*: Guardian, 17 March 1976. *Javanese woman*: Sun, 12 Feb 1988. *Philippines villagers*: Reveille, 11 May 1979. *Hapur battle*: Independent, 15 Feb 1992. *Philippines Catholics*: Mail on Sunday, 4 July 1993. *Faaite Islanders*: The Garden Island (Hawaii), 30 March 1990.

CHAPTER 14: THAT OL' BLACK MAGIC

Camus: S. Express, 7 March 1976, Guardian, 13 May, D. Mail, 14 May 1977. *Mpofu*: Houston Post, 27 Sept 1990. *Lu Zhihua*: New Straits Times, 4 Aug 1992. *Delamare*: S. Express, 23 April 1978. *Lebowa witch-burnings*: Guardian, 6 Jan + 7 Feb, D. Telegraph, 21 Feb 1984, etc. *Kgabi*: Guardian, 30 Nov 1978, Pretoria News, 8 + 20 June 1979. *Kazaalwa*: Victoria Times-Colonist, 16 Nov 1987. *Allison*: Independent, 19 Aug 1989. *Mangayanon*: E. Standard, 19 Sept, S.Telegraph, 22 Sept 1985. *Jamaican Pentecostalists*: S. Times, 25 June 1978. *Williams*: D. Express, 6 Aug 1974.

CHAPTER 15: THE ULTIMATE SACRIFICE

Godefray: D. Mirror, 24 Sept 1984. *Altun*: D. Telegraph, 28 Nov 1990. *Kuala Lumpur boy*: D. Mirror, 21 March 1984. *Sichuan farmer*: Independent, 24 March 1991. *Bayat*: Rocky Mountain News, 28 Nov 1992. *Mills*: Morning Post, 10 Feb 1933. *Magalhaes*: The Province, 23 + 27 Oct 1979. *Mtawara tribe*: D. News, 19 Feb 1923. *Sipche villagers*: D. Express, (date unknown) 1972. *Giri*: Indian Express, 6 March, Times of India, 7 March 1980. *Delhi girl*: D. Star, 26 Sept 1991. *Khatun*: Guardian, 19 July 1988. *Arellano*: AP wire, 10 Nov 1991.

CHAPTER 16: CANNIBALISM, COOKERY AND BLOOD-DRINKING

Ondanga: Sun, 28 April 1977. *Red Guards*: Observer, 10 Jan 1993. *Japanese soldiers*: Bangkok Post, 11 Aug 1992. *Wang Guang*: Straits Times, 23 March 1991. *Hao Ki*: AFP wire, 15 Jan 1994. *Cheng family*: Independent, 9 Oct 1986. *Harare cannibals*: Bangkok Post, 16 Oct 1992. *Wirjo*: D. Telegraph, 17 April 1987. *Bobo*: Bradford Telegraph & Argus, 17 Feb 1988. *Naragathavally*: D. Mirror, 28 March, D. Telegraph, 8 June, 1987. *Beerle*: Toronto Sun, 1 Oct 1989. *Baldock*: Victoria Times-Colonist, 16 Feb 1991. *John*: AFP wire, 15 April 1993. *Lenpeng*: S. People, 22 June 1975.

CHAPTER 17: FATAL FOOD

Villenti: People, 27 March 1991. *Rosales*: Independent, 15 Dec 1993. *Wettstein*: S. People, 25 Sept 1977. *Quinquandon*: D. Telegraph, 27 Nov 1979, etc. *Federici*: Weekend, 3 May 1978. *Mulhern*: N.Y. Post, 14 Nov 1988. *Merry*: D. Mirror, 27 July 1989, etc. *Marseilles worker*: D. Record, 15 July 1993. *LaRose*: Times-Reporter, 11 April 1991. *Katash*: D. Mirror, 27 Oct 1992. *Bangkok man*: Guardian, 7 Oct 1985. *Ohisson*: D. Star, 21 Oct 1993.

CHAPTER 18: CLAWS AND PAWS

Hall: National Register, 30 June 1811. *Fernando*: Sun, 9 March 1988. *Korean fisherman*: Shropshire Star, 4 June 1979. *Cista*: Sun, 25 July 1983. *Obidos ferry-boat*: D. Star, 21 Sept 1981. *Godavari river-boat*: N.Y. Post, 21 Feb 1991. *Maghnia boys*: AFP wire, 4 May 1992. *Nabi*: D. Telegraph, 15 June 1981. *Cawthorne*: D. Telegraph, 21 Oct 1993. *Hatibu*: Independent, 24 Dec 1990. *Scrimmin*: D. Star, 5 Oct 1992. *Montana woman*: E. News, 29 Aug 1979. *Meech*: Denver Post, 17 July 1993. *Dankert*: Sun, 1 Feb 1982. *Ahani*: AP wire, 24 April 1990. *Hussein*: Jakarta Post, 24 Nov 1984. *Beukes*: Seychelles Nation, 27 Feb 1993. *Trincomalee woman*: S. Express, 1 July 1984. *Malaysian man*: E. Standard, 12 Jan 1978. *Pakistani man*: D. Telegraph, 3 Sept 1984.

CHAPTER 19: ROTTEN SHOTS

Boyer: Sun, 2 Nov 1990. *Ilic*: S. People, 22 Oct 1978. *Japanese housewife*: Halifax Evening Courier, 6 Dec 1993. *New Zealand farmer's son*: D. Telegraph, 13 Nov 1988. *Duncan*: BBC Wildlife, March 1992. *Namibian Motorist*: Bild Zeitung, 10 Aug 1989. *Lewis*: D. Star, 4 Nov 1991. *Benitez*: D. Mirror, 1992. *Tate*: Laredo Morning Times, 10 June 1988. *Ribolla*: S. Express, 5 April 1981. *Lovell*: Baltimore Sun, 15 Dec 1987. *Fagny*: D. Record, 12 Oct 1991. *Spanu*: Sun, 28 Feb 1992. *Baschuz*: Guardian, 19 Aug 1992. *Thai teacher*: D. Mirror, 17 Nov 1993.

CHAPTER 20: MYSTERIES AND MURDERS

Orsini: S. Express, 29 March 1981. *Burnett*: Newark Star Ledger, 20 Dec 1992. *Przewozny*: D. Mirror, 18 Aug 1966. *Marseilles Mystery*: S. Express, 16 May 1976. *Ahmand*: S. Express, 31 Aug 1980. *Dartmoor man*: S. Express, 3 July 1977. *Marten*: S. Mirror, 23 Aug 1981. *Green + Mannon*: N.Y. Post, 21 Feb 1980. *Burns*: Victoria Times-Colonist, 9 Sept 1987.

CHAPTER 21: FUNERAL FOLLIES

Thanjavur priest: N.Y. Post, 16 Jan 1991. *Mohammad*: San Jose Mercury News, 5 May 1992. *Vallefiorita brothers*: Scotsman, 5 Sept 1986. *Gaenheim woman*: D. Record, 14 Jan 1986. *Bujumbura hitch-hikers*: D. Telegraph, 13 Feb 1980. *Volkering*: Chillicothe Gazette, 14 Jan 1989. *Dumelow*: D. Star, 24 Jan 1991. *Richards*: Sun, 14 Dec 1989. *Overton*: D. Mirror, 8 March 1990. *Metcalf*: Guardian, 14 July 1982. *Paraiba undertakers*: D. Telegraph, 28 July 1992.